THE COMPLETE

Soapmaker

THE COMPLETE
Soapmaker

Tips, Techniques & Recipes
for Luxurious Handmade Soaps

Norma Coney

Sterling Publishing Co., Inc. New York
A Sterling/Lark Book

The Complete Soapmaker:
Tips, Techniques, and Recipes for Luxurious Handmade Soaps
is dedicated to my husband, Denny.

Editor: **CHRIS RICH**
Art Director and Photo Stylist: **CHRIS BRYANT**
Production: **CHRIS BRYANT**
Photography: **EVAN BRACKEN**

Library of Congress Cataloging-in-Publication Data

Coney, Norma J., 1955-
    The complete soapmaker: tips, techniques, and recipes for luxurious handmade soaps / by Norma Coney
    p.   cm.
    "A Sterling/Lark book."
    Includes index.
    ISBN 0-8069-4868-X
    1. Soap.   I. Title
TP991.C66   1955
668'.124—dc20   95-40311
                                        CIP

10 9

A Sterling/Lark Book

Published by Sterling Publishing Company, Inc.
    387 Park Avenue South, New York, N.Y. 10016

Produced by Altamont Press, Inc.
    50 College Street, Asheville, NC 28801

Distributed in Canada by Sterling Publishing,
    c/o Canadian Manda Group, One Atlantic Avenue, Suite 105, Toronto, Ontario, Canada M6K 3E7

Distributed in Great Britain and Europe by Cassell PLC,
    Wellington House, 125 Strand, London, England WC2R OBB

Distributed in Australia by Capricorn Link (Australia) Pty Ltd.,
    P.O. Box 6651, Baulkham Hills Business Centre, NSW, Australia 2153

Every effort has been made to ensure that all the information in this book is accurate. However, due to differing conditions, tools, and individual skills, the publisher cannot be responsible for any injuries, losses, or other damages that may result from the use of the information in this book.

Table of Contents

An Introduction to Soap Making

Making soap is one of those hobbies that almost always elicits curiosity. When people ask me why on earth I make my own soap, my answer is simple. I started because I needed to make ends meet at home. Along the way, however, I developed a wonderful hobby, one which has allowed me to make and give away dozens of beautiful, useful gifts and to learn about and grow the herbs that I use as additives. I haven't bought a bar of commercial soap in years.

Through the soap-making classes that I now teach, I've also made many friends. The cooperation and camaraderie that develop in these classes are special; they haven't been quite as evident in other classes I've taught. When I ask my students why they think this is true, they say it's because making soap is innately interesting. My own theory is that soap-making students also develop a sense of "togetherness" because they realize that we all share the same predicament: We all learn by making the same mistakes!

With the help of this book, you'll first discover how to make what I call *basic soaps*—simple soaps, each with its own distinctive characteristics—which you'll slice into square or rectangular bars. These bars don't require much time to create, can be tailored in content to suit your type of skin, and are practical soaps for family use.

Then you'll discover how to make *hand-milled soaps*—basic soaps which have been grated, remelted, and molded or cut into bars. Though hand-milled soaps take longer to make than basic soaps, many can rival the fancy bars sold at fine stores. They're harder than basic soap bars, they last longer, and they're easily scented and "filled" with a wide range of skin-friendly additives. What's more, some hand-milled bars can be made in two separate stages. Several of the basic soaps described in this book can be grated, dried, and left until you're ready to mill them, so you'll never feel pressed to process an entire batch at one time. Best of all, hand-milled soaps can be poured into individual molds to make fancy gift bars.

As you make your first few batches of soap—a process which will take several weeks—your soap-making skills will evolve, and as they do, you'll discover and create new combinations of fragrances and additives to thrill those on the receiving end of your new hobby.

Making either basic or hand-milled soaps at home is economical. Once you've purchased the inexpensive equipment you need, your soap will pay for itself, and in time, you'll become so adept at molding attractive individual bars that you may never have to buy another gift again. There are ways, of course, to make this craft expensive. Indulging in high-priced scent oils and additives is one! Most people, however, are satisfied with the many reasonably priced and rewarding alternatives.

Don't be discouraged if you feel a bit overwhelmed at first. I've been a student, too, so I'm entirely sympathetic. You aren't a chemist, but neither am I, and I know that you don't need to be one to be successful at soap making. What you do need is faith in yourself—and patience. Before long, you'll have mastered a wonderful new hobby and will reap its many rewards.

An Overview

Soap making isn't terribly complex, but its stages can be confusing for beginners. In this section, you'll find a description of the soap-making process and an outline that will acquaint you with the sequence of steps involved. Think of this overview of upcoming chapters as a mental file cabinet into which you'll be dropping more detailed information as you read the rest of the book. You'll also find some definitions of soap-making terms. By familiarizing yourself with these terms, you'll make your new hobby much easier to learn.

WHAT SOAP IS AND HOW IT'S MADE

Interestingly, few people know what soap really is. Several of the cleansing bars that you buy at the store and use in the shower or bath, for example, are detergents—and not soaps at all. The same holds true for many liquid hand "soaps" and shampoos.

Soaps, unlike detergents, are made by combining lye, animal fats and/or vegetable oils, and water in a process known as *saponification*. Detergents, on the other hand, contain petroleum distillates rather than fats or oils.

Soap can be made in several different ways. In the *cold process* method described in this book, saponification takes several days to complete, and glycerin, a natural byproduct of saponification, remains in the finished soap.

In the *boiling* or *kettle method*, a process used by industry pioneers in the mid-nineteenth century, heated steam was directed through the soap mixture, and after saponification took place, salt was added to the vat, causing the soap (known as *neat soap*) to rise to the surface and the glycerin to sink to the bottom. The glycerin was then collected, purified, and sold separately. Additional ingredients were added to complete the soap.

Today, commercial soaps are made by what is known as the *continuous process*, in which saponification takes place while the ingredients are under pressure in a large vat. As its name suggests, this method permits raw ingredients to be added continuously to one end of the vat while soap is continuously removed from the other.

The high pressure in the vat, combined with high temperatures and the addition of a catalyst, causes almost immediate saponification of the ingredients. After saponification, the soap is often exposed to hydrogen, which further hardens it. The glycerin is removed from most commercial soaps. The continuous process also makes it possible to produce reasonably high-quality soaps with lower grade fats and oils.

The various soaps described in this book are different. How? The basic soaps that you will make are created with high-quality natural ingredients. In fact, unless you choose to incorporate purchased dyes or synthetic fragrance oils, many of these soaps can be made with nothing other than natural ingredients. Your soaps will feel "earthy" and will be much kinder to your skin than commercial soaps because the glycerin which remains in them is a natural emollient. By making your own soap, you'll be guaranteeing your family and friends a superior product, and you'll have a great time doing it, too!

Terms You'll Need to Know

Abrasives

Gritty substances which, when used in soaps, serve to scrub away dirt, outer skin cells, and excess oils.

Additives

Ingredients which are usually added to soaps during the milling process. Additives impart special qualities to soaps.

Astringents

Substances which, when used in soaps, tighten and close the pores in skin, hence making one's skin feel smoother.

Basic Soaps

Simple soaps in which proportions of fats and/or oils are manipulated to produce varying degrees of mildness and different lathering qualities. Additives – ingredients which are not necessary for saponification – are not usually included in basic soap recipes.

Cold Process Soap Making

A method of creating handmade soaps which takes place at relatively low temperatures.

Detergents

Defined in this book as cleansers in which petroleum distillates take the place of animal fats and/or vegetable oils.

Emollients

Substances which soften the skin. Glycerin, waxes, and oils are all effective emollients.

Essential Oils

High-quality oils distilled directly from plant materials.

Fixatives

Substances which stabilize fragrances so that they will not dissipate as quickly.

Fragrance Oils

Synthetically produced oils which mimic the aromas of essential oils.

Hand-Cut Soaps

Square or rectangular bars made by cutting large blocks of basic or milled soaps into sections.

Hand-Milled Soaps

Soaps made by grating basic soaps and remelting them with water. Additional ingredients are often included during this process.

Rendering

A cooking process during which impurities in animal fats are removed to yield *tallow* – a pure fat suitable for making soap or candles.

Saponification

The process by which soap is formed. Occurs when fats and/or oils are combined with an alkali (in this case, lye).

Using This Book

To get some idea of what to expect from each chapter in this book and of the sequence of steps you'll be taking as you make soap, take a good look at the outline in this section.

ONE TIP FOR BEGINNERS: *Before you start to make soap, always read the instructions carefully. Then imagine yourself working through each and every step before you actually take it; you'll have a much easier time with your first few batches if you do.*

Chapter One Get acquainted with the equipment you'll need.

Chapter Two Familiarize yourself with common ingredients.

Chapter Three Learn some basic safety rules.

Chapter Four Render your suet into tallow.

Chapter Five Select a basic soap recipe and gather your equipment and ingredients.

Weigh the lye and the fats and/or oils.

Mix the lye solution.

Melt the fats and/or oils over heat.

Equalize the temperatures of the lye solution and the fats and/or oils at 100°F (38°C).

Pour the lye solution into the fats and/or oils, and stir.

Pour the warm soap into a primary mold.

Wrap the mold in insulating materials.

Allow the big block of basic soap to dry in the primary mold.

You'll start by making a batch of basic soap, using one of the recipes in Chapter Five.

The finished block of basic soap can be cut into bars, or . . .

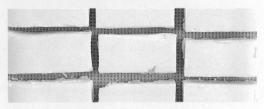

. . . grated and melted to make hand-milled soaps.

Specialty soaps, such as shampoos, transluscent bars, and marbled soaps, are great fun to make and give away.

HAND-CUT BASIC SOAPS

Chapter Five   Remove the block of basic soap from the mold, and score the block to prepare it for making hand-cut bars.

When the block has partially dried, slice it into finished bars of basic soap.

Allow the hand-cut bars to cure.

HAND-MILLED SOAPS

Chapter Six   Read instructions for making hand-milled soaps.

Chapter Seven   Select a hand-milled soap recipe.

Chapter Six   Cut the block of basic soap into chunks.

Grate the chunks.

Mix the grated soap with water and melt it over heat.

Mix in additives, fragrances, and/or dyes, as specified in your selected hand-milled soap recipe.

Pour the soap into molds.

Remove the individual soaps from the molds and allow the soaps to cure.

SPECIALTY SOAPS

Chapter Eight   Select a specialty soap recipe.

Follow instructions for making that specialty soap.

FINAL TOUCHES

Chapter Nine   Learn to identify and solve soap-making problems.

Chapter Ten   Learn how to apply decals and how to wrap, store, and display your completed soaps.

Chapter One:
Equipment and Supplies

Making soap doesn't require a workshop filled with equipment; many of the necessary items may already be in your kitchen. Others, such as a scale and thermometers, you'll probably need to purchase.

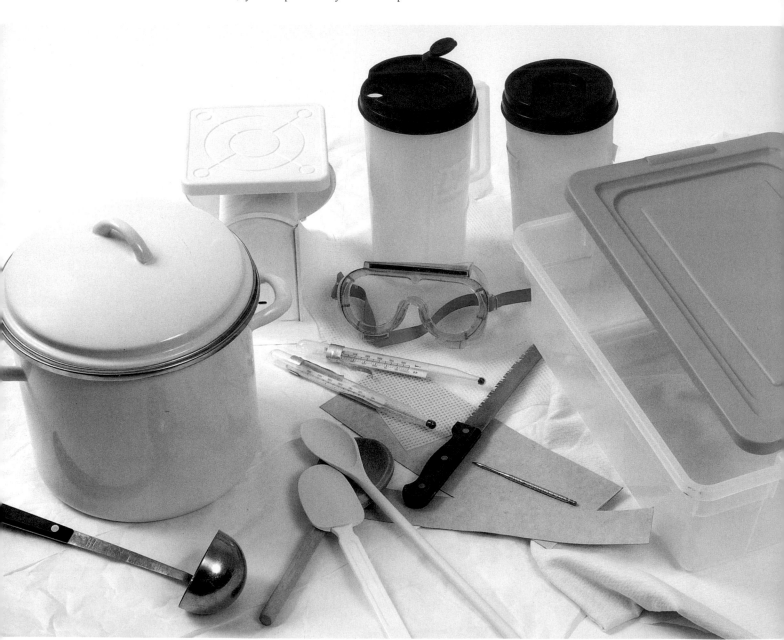

Kitchen Scale

Your scale needn't be expensive or fancy, but try to find one that can be readjusted to zero each time you use it. This feature will allow you to weigh your ingredients right into the soap pot by placing the pot on the scale, setting the scale at zero, adding the ingredient, weighing it, resetting the scale at zero, adding and weighing the next ingredient, and so on.

If you can't find or afford a scale of this type, any small scale that will measure up to 5 pounds (2.3 kg) will work, although you'll need to measure your ingredients individually before adding them to the soap pot.

A small postal scale will also come in handy, as you'll sometimes need one to weigh small amounts.

Soap Pot

Your batches of soap must be mixed in either an unchipped enamel or stainless-steel kettle; lye will corrode most other materials. This vessel should be 8 quarts (7.6 l) or larger in size. Smaller pots may hold your batch of soap, but they won't leave enough room for stirring. If you plan to purchase a pot rather than recycle one from your household, select one that is deep and narrow rather than shallow and wide. Soap made in deeper pots will require less stirring.

Two Plastic Pitchers

These pitchers, used for mixing and pouring the lye solution, should have pouring spouts, removable lids that either snap or screw on tightly, and handles that are securely attached. Each should hold 2 quarts (1.9 l). Because the lye solution that is mixed in them will heat up to 200°F (93°C), the pitchers should also be "dishwasher safe," or the plastic may melt.

Do not use metal or glass pitchers. Metals may react with the lye in your soaps, and glass, besides being too slippery to handle safely when it's wet, is likely to crack when it's subjected to the high temperatures of lye solutions.

Long-Handled Wooden or Plastic Spoon

You'll be stirring the caustic lye solution with this spoon, so be sure that its handle is indeed long. Plan on reserving the spoon for soap making only, and keep in mind that lye will eventually chew up wooden spoons. Recycling a household spoon is fine, but don't use one stained with your favorite spaghetti sauce, or the color will transfer to your soap!

Two Kitchen Thermometers

Each thermometer must be capable of registering temperatures as low as 100°F (38°C). The probe end, which will be inserted into the soap or lye, must be made of glass or stainless steel; lye will destroy aluminum probes. For your own convenience, purchase thermometers with hooks so you can attach them to the side of the soap pot or pitcher. This way, you won't need to reach into the oils or lye to read the thermometer. Inexpensive candy and deep-fry thermometers work well.

Be sure you know how to read your thermometers before you use them. Many a student has ruined her soap by misreading a thermometer—or by assuming that it could be read in the same way as other thermometers on the market.

Safety Glasses or Goggles

Protect your eyes by wearing safety glasses or goggles whenever you're pouring or mixing your soap.

Rubber or Plastic Gloves

You must wear gloves to protect your hands and your lower arms from caustic lye and from hot liquid soap.

Wooden or Stainless Steel Ladle

A ladle will prove useful when you're transferring soap from the soap pot to a mold.

Sharp Knife

You'll use this knife to cut up suet or beef fat for rendering, and for slicing bars of finished soap.

Large, Clear Plastic Container with Lid

Known to soap makers as the *primary mold*, this container will hold your liquid basic soap and should be 12 quarts (11.4 l) or more in size. Using a container made of clear plastic will enable you to spot any problems with your soap before you remove the soap from it. Opaque containers, on the other hand, may hide lye that has failed to combine properly with the fats and/or oils. Attempting to remove soap that has separated in this fashion can be dangerous when you're not prepared to deal with it, as the caustic lye may splash onto your skin.

A clear plastic tub with a snap-on lid will work well, and if it's rectangular or square, you'll end up with a large block of soap from which rectangular or square bars can be cut quite easily.

To improve the final appearance of your finished hand-cut bars, make sure that your primary mold has a smooth inner surface and square corners. Avoid the use of liners such as plastic wrap, which tend to wrinkle.

Old Blanket or Towel

As your warm soap sets up in the primary mold, it must be insulated, or it will cool too quickly. Wrapping an old blanket or towel around your soap-filled primary mold will help the soap to cool slowly. If you wish, you may substitute pieces of foam rubber, rigid polystyrene foam, or a few old pillows.

Thin Cardboard

In order to slice your soap into rectangular or square bars, you'll need to make templates out of thin cardboard. An empty cereal box works well for this purpose.

Plastic Needlepoint Screen, Freezer Paper, or Butcher Paper

After you slice your block of basic soap into bars, you will need to set the bars onto a sheet of one of these materials to cure. Don't cure these bars or milled and molded bars on color-impregnated materials such as cardboard, as the soap may absorb the colors.

Kitchen Grater

To make hand-milled soaps, you will need to grate a block of basic soap. An inexpensive, rectangular kitchen grater, with its four grating surfaces, is perfect for this task. Use the grating surface with the largest holes.

Food Processor (Optional)

This kitchen appliance is very useful for processing suet before rendering.

Sheet of Rigid Plastic (Optional)

If you envision yourself making many batches of soap, purchase a thick, 2-foot by 3-foot (61.0 by 91.4 cm) piece of transparent, rigid plastic to serve as a cutting surface. A sheet of cardboard will serve the same purpose, but

it obviously won't last as long and may discolor the soap. Even flat plastic lids will work.

Sieve or Colander

When rendering suet or beef fat, you will need to separate out any debris from the dissolved fat by straining it through this kitchen utensil.

Stainless Steel Pots

A couple of pots that are smaller than your soap pot will be necessary when you're making small batches of hand-milled soaps. Your large soap pot might work for this purpose, but is likely to prove a bit cumbersome and may be so large that your soap will scorch during milling.

Soap Molds

Perhaps nothing is as important to the appearance of finished hand-milled soaps as the molds you use when making them. Although many molds will yield serviceable bars of soap, there's something special about an extra fancy-looking bar. Searching for soap molds that please you is well worth your while, and fortunately, molds are more available today than they have been in the past.

As you'll soon discover, however, molds made specifically for soaps are few and far between. The molds that you'll probably use as substitutes fall into two categories: molds that were made for other purposes, such as candy or candle making; and molds that weren't made to be molds at all.

Manufactured molds such as candy and candle molds tend to be much fancier than "found" molds, and their shapes are usually best suited for making guest soaps and smaller bars. These molds are available from many craft-supply stores and candy- or candle-making suppliers.

You'll even find that some of these sources provide soap-making molds as well. Frog, bear, snail, shell, and cat shapes will appeal to people who prefer the natural look. Cars, Christmas trees, and comic-strip characters will probably please folks who enjoy themes. All these molds are fun to work with and give very professional-looking results.

As entertaining as these smaller molds tend to be, most people also long for hefty bars to take into the shower at the end of the day. The desire for larger soaps will send you off on a search for the second—often

SUGGESTED SOAP MOLDS

- Old-fashioned aluminum gelatin molds
- Microwave containers
- Food containers with individual compartments
- Candy molds, available in a huge array of shapes and sizes
- Plastic ice-cream cups with fluted sides
- Candle molds
- Maple-sugar molds
- Plastic "eggs" used to hold pantyhose
- Small plastic drawer organizers
- Individual tart pans
- Sardine cans

SOAP MOLD SPECIFICATIONS

■ Plastic and stainless steel are the best mold materials. Glass and china molds are acceptable as a last resort, but the soap in them won't be easy to extract, and mold breakage is always a concern. The small plastic containers in which some types of cheeses and dairy spreads are packaged make great molds for larger bars and can be found in both round and rectangular shapes. Aluminum molds are risky only if your soap hasn't cured properly and still has actively caustic lye in it; they work very well with properly cured soaps.

■ Mold materials must be able to withstand the high temperatures of hot soap. Empty plastic cookie trays, for example, sometimes have wonderful designs on their bottom surfaces, but beware! These nondurable trays will melt or deform when soap is poured into them.

■ Flexible molds are preferable to ones that are completely rigid, as the bars will be easier to remove.

■ Try to be practical when it comes to the size and depth of the mold. Though a shape may take your fancy, if the mold is too shallow or too small, the soap that you mold in it will just end up slipping down the drain. Also keep in mind that soap shrinks as it dries. Aim for variety in your soap-mold collection, and be sure to include some for making large bars, some for making medium-size hand soaps, and some small ones for making guest soaps.

■ The open end of any mold must be larger than the closed end, or the hardened soap will be trapped inside. Avoid straight-sided molds, or you'll end up having to pry the soap out with a knife, marring the bars as you do. Plastic juice containers, for example, just won't work, unless you're prepared to destroy the mold by cutting or peeling it away. Occasionally, soap makers do choose to treat their molds as disposable.

■ Select molds with enough detail on their inner surfaces to provide beautifully expressed soaps, and try a few basic molds before you invest a fortune in ones you may never use. Add to your collection when you're more experienced and know more about what you're looking for.

elusive—type of mold. These larger molds usually spend their first lifetimes holding cheese or ice cream, or impersonating microwave food containers. You, however, will recognize them for what they really are—soap molds!

You'll soon find yourself looking for potential molds everywhere you go, and when this happens, you'll know you're hooked on soap making. The potential number of undiscovered and unfulfilled soap molds is staggering. Only your creativity and imagination will limit the number you can find.

Chapter Two:
Ingredients

Because each ingredient lends a special characteristic to your finished soap, it's a good idea to familiarize yourself with common ingredients before you select a recipe. In this section, you'll find two lists: one of ingredients for basic soap recipes and one of ingredients for hand-milled soaps, including additives, fragrances, and dyes. Look for all these ingredients in grocery stores, health-food stores, and through herb-supply companies.

AN ASSORTMENT OF FATS AND OILS COMMONLY USED IN COLD-PROCESS SOAP MAKING

BASIC SOAP INGREDIENTS

Basic ingredients are those used in basic soap recipes—the recipes from which hand-cut basic soap bars are made.

Suet, the fat that surrounds the kidneys of cows, is the preferred ingredient for making tallow—the pure fat that results when suet or other fats are rendered (see Chapter Four). Purchase suet from the meat counter at your grocery store. Good-quality suet may vary slightly in color but should be white or slightly off-white in color rather than grey. Its texture should be firm and flaky. Refrigerate or freeze your suet until used.

Suet yields a hard tallow, one with which it's easy to work. Soaps made with suet are relatively mild.

Beef fat (the ordinary type) lacks the firm texture of suet and tends to be darker and more slippery to the touch. Because beef fat is softer than suet, the tallow it yields isn't as high in quality, so use suet whenever you can. Refrigerate or freeze beef fat until used.

Soaps made with beef fat are softer than soaps made with suet and can be difficult to work with.

Tallow is the pure fat that remains after suet or beef fat has been rendered to remove impurities such as sinew and meat (see Chapter Four). Refrigerate or freeze tallow until used.

Soaps made with large amounts of tallow are mild to the skin and hard to the touch. Suds from tallow soaps yield small creamy bubbles.

Lard is the rendered fat of pigs. One-pound (454 g) packages are often available in grocery-store dairy aisles. Refrigerate or freeze until used.

Soaps made with lard are quite mild to the skin and reasonably hard to the touch. They do not lather well, so lard is usually combined with other fats and/or oils.

Palm oil, expressed from certain types of palm, used to be widely available as a cooking oil, but for health reasons has fallen from favor. Palm oil colors include white, golden, orange, and nearly red. Although the color of the oil will affect the color of your soap, this effect lessens as the bars dry. Look for palm oil in stores that feature foods from the Middle East, Asia, and Africa, or through mail-order suppliers.

Soaps made with palm oil have rich, luxurious, long-lasting bubbles. Because these soaps are extra mild, they're especially suitable for use as facial soaps. Palm oil soaps do tend to be a bit soft and difficult to mold when milled. For the best results, mill as soon as possible.

Coconut oil, a white oil derived from the meat of the familiar coconut, is used widely in commercially produced soaps and candles. Although hard to the touch at room temperature, this oil melts readily when warmed. Look for coconut oil in Asian groceries, large grocery stores with Asian-food sections, and in health-food stores. You may also be able to obtain coconut oil through bakery-supply houses.

Because coconut oil is used to make commercial popcorn, it's sometimes sold by wholesalers as "popping oil." Coconut oil sold under this name may have been dyed to a yellowish orange tint. This color may transfer to your soap, but the scent will dissipate quickly.

Soaps made with coconut oil tend to dry the skin, so the recipes in this book call for limited quantities. Coconut oil creates moderately hard soaps and plenty of creamy lather.

Cocoa butter is derived from the seeds of the cacao tree and is separated out during the process of making cocoa. This hard, rich oil is also used to make candy. Look for cocoa butter wherever candy-making supplies are sold or at your local pharmacy.

Cocoa butter improves the overall consistency of the soap, making it creamy and hard. Because the butter is an emollient, it also softens the skin and makes it smooth.

Vegetable shortening makes an adequate substitute for animal fats if you have an aversion to animal-based products.

Soaps made with this shortening are usually soft and low in bubbles, so shortening is combined with other oils in our recipes.

Castor oil is expressed from the seed of the castor bean plant. You'll find this oil, which is thick and medicinal in nature, at your local pharmacy. In our recipes, small amounts of castor oil are used as supplements to other oils.

Castor oil adds richness and mildness to soaps.

Olive oil comes in several grades, all of which are suitable for soap making.

This oil makes a very hard and brittle soap, which dries quickly and lathers readily and profusely. Olive oil soaps are mild, long-lasting, and of very high quality.

Vegetable oils are often blended oils and usually contain about 10 percent olive oil and a 90 percent combination of corn, soy, and peanut oils. Vegetable oils are very inexpensive and give generally good results in soap making.

Blended vegetable oils yield softer soaps than olive oil alone. They do not dry as quickly, and they lather well.

Rendered kitchen fats—fats left over after frying meat or fats skimmed from soup stocks—are what your grandmother probably saved for her soap-making ventures. I keep my drippings in a coffee can in the refrigerator, an option my grandmother didn't have! Render these fats just as you would render suet.

The quality of soaps made with these fats will vary, depending on the origins of the fats used. Pork, beef, and lamb fat can be used, but soaps made with them will never match soaps made with refined oils or pure rendered fats. Avoid using high proportions of chicken fat, as it will make your soap too soft.

Using Fats from Other Animals

Students have asked me whether they can substitute other animal fats for those recommended in my recipes. Though I've never tried doing so, my common sense tells me that any animal fat can be rendered to make tallow. The harder the fat, the better it will be for soap making. Mutton fat, for example, is hard and of high quality, and has been used in parts of the world where beef fat is hard to come by.

Lye (also known as *sodium hydroxide*) is a caustic alkaline substance, which makes soap when it's combined with fats and/or oils. Once created by dripping water through wood ashes, lye is now manufactured commercially, so its strength is dependably consistent. Purchase lye at grocery or hardware stores (it's often placed next to the drain cleaners), and exercise extreme caution when using it!

Lye soaps are characteristically hard.

HAND-MILLED SOAP INGREDIENTS

For home-based soap makers, nothing is quite as exciting as individualizing hand-milled soaps by including additives, fragrances, and colors.

These ingredients are mixed in when a batch of basic soap is remelted to make milled soap. (Note, however, that basic soaps may also be milled without adding extra ingredients.)

Additives

Additives are substances which not only alter the overall look of a given soap but which also lend their own special qualities to it. These substances range from honey, a wonderful skin softener, to oatmeal, the gentle scrubbing qualities of which enhance facial and body soaps.

Almond meal, which consists of the finely ground kernels of blanched almonds, acts to unclog skin pores and absorb excess oil from the skin.

Almond oil (sweet) is the debittered cosmetic oil derived from almonds and contains protein and several vitamins. Well known for its ability to soften the skin, this oil is used in many cosmetics, soaps, and perfumes.

Aloe vera gel, a healing substance extracted from the aloe plant, is used worldwide to heal burns and skin abrasions.

Althaea roots (marshmallow roots), from the plant *Althaea officinalis*, are used widely in bronchial treatments and also serve as wonderful skin softeners. The plant is easily grown in the garden, but the roots may also be purchased at many health-food stores.

Anise oil, a medicinal oil extracted from the seeds of *Pimpinella anisum*, is believed to be attractive to fish! It's included in our recipe for Fisherman's Soap (see Chapter Seven).

Apricots have been used for centuries in cosmetic preparations, as they have skin-softening properties and are high in mineral salts and vitamins. Fresh or dried apricots may be used in soaps.

Avocados, available at your grocery store, were once used as an aphrodisiac. We make no guarantees on that score, but the oils have an ancient history of use in cosmetics.

Benzoin is a resin that acts as a fixative for fragrances in soaps and as a preservative. Use benzoin in its powdered form.

Borax, a mineral which contains sodium, is valued in cosmetics for its ability to soften and disinfect the skin. The sodium in high concentrations of borax may curdle your soap, however, so use this mineral sparingly.

Bran is the broken outer husk of any grain and acts as a mild abrasive in facial soaps. You'll find bran at health-food or grocery stores.

Buttermilk is the sour liquid left after butterfat is separated from milk or cream. Always use the freshest buttermilk possible and include it only in basic soaps which are hard in consistency, as it tends to soften soaps considerably.

Calendula flowers have a long history as skin softeners. They are very soothing to sensitive and dry skins and are excellent additions to facial soaps. Use the petals only, either fresh or dried, first removing them from the heads and discarding any seeds.

Carrots are high in vitamin A and many other vitamins, and their essential oil also contains a good bit of vitamin E. Purchase bright orange, fresh carrots for use in soap.

Chamomile flowers, from the *Anthemus nobilis* plant, add a slightly astringent quality to soaps. This herb is commonly sold as a tea; the crushed flower heads may be used straight from the tea bags. Do avoid chamomile if you're allergic to pollens!

Cinnamon makes a dark soap with a pleasant spicy aroma. It is mildly abrasive to the skin, has gentle antiseptic properties, and adds longevity and character to soap lather. Use ground cinnamon only.

Clay—also sold as *French clay* or *facial clay*—is widely used for cosmetic purposes because it draws out and absorbs oil from the skin. Soaps made with clay are therefore somewhat drying. Red, green, or beige clays are available from many health-food stores.

Cloves are antiseptic, but can be irritating, so use this spice only in small amounts. Use oil of cloves or commercially ground cloves; grinding whole cloves will damage plastic blenders or plastic food processors.

Cocoa butter is an emollient and adds soothing properties to any soap. The rich, solid oil is white and will not affect the color of your soap.

Coffee is used in soaps to absorb odors from the skin. Use fresh unbrewed grounds.

Cornmeal absorbs oils and has long been used for its mildly abrasive qualities, which help to unclog skin pores. Either white or yellow cornmeal will work well.

Cucumbers, when liquefied and added to soaps, act as mild cleansers and as astringents.

Flowers of sulfur have been used as an antiseptic and as a remedy for mild skin problems for many years.

Ginger, when included in soaps, warms the skin. Use it sparingly and in ground form only.

Glycerin is a sweet, syrupy, colorless by-product of commercial soap making and acts as a soothing skin emollient. Our cold-process basic soaps retain their natural glycerin and can be further enhanced by adding more glycerin when they are milled.

Honey has been used as an emollient for centuries and makes an excellent addition to soap. Use any raw honey of your choice. Because honey will soften soaps during the milling process, select a basic soap recipe that yields a hard soap.

Kelp, often sold as "sea vegetables," includes several types of large leaf-like algae, all rich in iodine, vitamins, and minerals. The algae add a slippery feel and mild ocean scent to soap. Purchase kelp in powdered form.

Kiwis, the fruit of *Actinidia chinensis*, are widely grown in New Zealand, where they're esteemed for their medicinal properties. They are also available in the produce sections of many grocery stores. Kiwis contain protein and mineral salts and are rich in vitamins.

Lanolin (also called *wool wax*) is the wax taken from sheep's wool and is unsurpassed in its moisturizing and skin-softening properties. Use it with caution, however, as it's also a common skin-contact allergen. Lanolin should be used in its raw state, in very low concentrations.

Lavender flowers add a nice touch to lavender-scented soaps and help to hold the scent as well. Use the blossoms fresh or dried and as finely ground as possible.

Lemons can be incorporated as juice (fresh or reconstituted), as grated peels, or in the form of dried granules. Renowned as a food and cosmetic ingredient, lemons are also medicinal; the oil in the peel is antibacterial in nature, and the peels contain high levels of vitamin C.

Lettuce contains many vitamins and makes a very mild soap. Use any variety of clean, fresh lettuce.

Milk (cow or goat) has been used since ancient times as a natural cleanser. When using raw goat's milk, make sure it's as fresh as possible. Instant powdered milk may be substituted for fresh or bottled cow's milk. Select a basic soap that is hard in consistency, as dairy products will soften any soap to which they are added.

Myrrh is the gum derived from *Commiphora myrrha*, a tree native to the Middle East. It has been valued since antiquity for its antibacterial qualities. Purchase myrrh in its powdered form.

Nutmeg is a fragrant spice which adds zest to lemon in soap recipes. Use nutmeg in its powdered form.

Oatmeal has long been used to soothe sensitive or irritated skin. Select long-cooking or rolled oats for soaps; quick-cooking or instant oats may thicken your soap too quickly, turning it into a rubbery glob that will be nearly impossible to mold. Grind the oatmeal into moderate-sized pieces in a blender or food processor.

Pectin, sold in powdered form at most grocery stores, will come in handy when you make shampoos, as it will keep the liquid shampoo from separating.

Peruvian balsam (also known as *balsam of Peru* and as *tolu*) is obtained from *Myroxylon balsamum*, a tree native to parts of South America. This thick, sticky liquid has a warm fragrance and is a common ingredient in cosmetics of all types. Use in liquid form.

Pumice is ground volcanic rock. It varies in color from white to almost black and is used in soaps as an abrasive. Use only pumice that has been finely ground.

Rosemary leaves, from the *Rosmarinus officinalis* plant, are very fragrant and have a mildly astringent effect on the skin. Use in powdered form.

Rose water is an emollient liquid made from commercial rose oil; it lends to soap its gentle fragrance, softening properties, and in some recipes, color.

Rosin, the finely powdered residue left after distillation of pine resins, helps bars of soap to retain their shape and produces large amounts of lather. Mix the powder with vegetable oil (any type will do) before adding it to the soap.

Sage (*Salvia officinalis*) is a pungent spice which has antibacterial, astringent, and antibacterial qualities. Use sage in its powdered form.

Sand, which is used as an abrasive in soap, must be clean and completely free of debris. Play sand, used in play boxes and available at many home centers, is suitable.

Strawberries contain several acids (including citric, tartaric, salicylic, and ascorbic) that make them effective as skin tighteners. These fruits are also high in Vitamin C and have been used cosmetically as a skin whitener. Use fresh strawberries when possible; frozen berries will also work, but do drain off and discard the syrup.

Sweet birch oil (from the *Betula alba* tree) has been used for years in Northern Europe to soothe skin afflictions such as eczema. In Scandinavia, people use birch twigs to flog their bodies after taking saunas. By jumping into icy water afterwards, they effectively trap the birch oil in their skin pores. You may find it easier to include the oil in your soap!

Tea tree oil is a healing oil derived from the tree *Melaleuca alternifolia*. Use in essential oil form.

Vitamin E oil has been used for many years to soothe the skin and prevent wrinkles. Use in undiluted form only.

Wheat germ, the inner germ of the wheat kernel, contains an oil which is purported to be excellent for the skin. The mildly abrasive germ and emollient oil are often used in facial and body soaps. Purchase either the germ or the oil from a health-food store or grocery store.

Witch hazel is a mildly astringent liquid distilled from the small tree of the same name. It cleanses the skin and closes the pores.

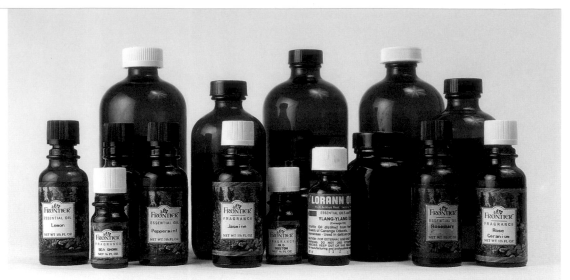

Fragrances

Scents will set your soaps apart from the crowd and will add yet another level of sophistication to your craft. Two cautions are in order, however. First, use scents sparingly; excessive amounts may cause skin irritations. If you have skin problems or a history of allergies, always perform a skin test (see page 29) before using these in your soaps. Second, never ingest either essential oils or fragrance oils unless the label tells you that it's safe to do so.

Essential oils, absolute oils, and resin oils are all perfect for scenting soaps. Unlike many other types of oils, they're extracted from individual plant sources and are very potent, so they often last longer and scent more material per ounce or gram than synthetic scents.

Fragrance oils, commonly used in potpourri, are made synthetically. If you aren't satisfied with the single scents offered by pure essential oils, these are for you. They're often almost as potent as essential oils and are available in a wide range of fragrances, from apple blossom to Christmas-scent combinations.

Beware of inexpensive oils of any type; these are often diluted or adulterated with extenders. Although they may look and even smell good in the bottle, they won't measure up to high-quality oils. Also avoid fragrances which contain alcohol, such as perfumes and after-shave lotions. These will evaporate quickly and will sometimes curdle the soap.

Choosing scents is largely a matter of personal taste and budget. Some scents, such as lavender, have long traditions as soap fragrances. Others, such as holiday or seasonal blends, are less traditional but are nevertheless quite appealing. Use any scent that you like, but keep in mind that some tend to be faint. When possible, test by sniffing! If you're ordering through the mail, ask the supplier which scents are the strongest, as these will be your best bets. Unbelievably good deals are rare; you're more likely to get what you pay for.

Traditional soap-making fragrances:

Almond
Apple
Cinnamon
Clove
Jasmine
Lavender
Lemon
Lilac
Orange blossom
Patchouli
Peach
Peppermint
Pine
Rose
Rose geranium
Sandalwood
Sassafras
Strawberry
Vanilla
Vetivert
Ylang ylang

Fixatives

Fixatives are substances that "fix" scents, helping them to retain their full fragrance in perfumed products. Powdered benzoin, vetivert, and myrrh all act as fixatives in scented milled soaps. These fixatives are available through mail-order suppliers and at some health-food stores.

Colors

Coloring your soaps, an easy step taken at the same time that fragrances are added, serves two purposes. The first is simply to make your soaps look more attractive. Colored soaps can be coordinated to accent bathroom decor, for example, and will make lovely gifts, too. The second reason to color your soaps is to help distinguish one soap recipe or scent from another. By keeping a record of the color you choose for each recipe, you'll be able to identify each soap at a glance.

Although there aren't any hard and fixed soap-making color rules to follow, pastel soaps do tend to look more natural than those in harsh primary colors. Also remember that adding colors isn't always necessary, as many additives will contribute their own colors to soaps.

When using dyes in soap, keep two rules in mind. First, the suds produced when the dyed soap is used should always be white. Test a bar from each batch. If your dyed soaps produce colored suds, discard them, as there's a good chance that these colors will be transferred to your towels, clothing, and skin! Second, dyed soaps should never be used to bathe infants. If you intend to give dyed soaps away as gifts, be sure to include in your gift package a prominent warning to this effect.

Several types of dye are available for soap making. Candle dyes and regular fabric dyes are the most commonly used. Food dyes may also be used, but with less satisfactory results.

Candle dye comes in small concentrated blocks of wax. To use these, place one block and two tablespoons (30 ml) of vegetable oil in a small saucepan and melt over low heat. After the block has dissolved in the oil and just before your grated and remelted basic soap is ready to pour into molds, gradually add just enough of the dye and oil as is necessary to yield the shade you desire. Stir thoroughly to ensure that the dye is dispersed throughout the liquid soap. Then store the remaining dye in a small jar.

Liquid fabric dyes, which are available in a wider range of colors than are candle dyes, are convenient, easy to use, and can be purchased at most supermarkets. These dyes are sodium-based, however, and should never be used by people who are sensitive to sodium or sodium compounds.

Purchase liquid fabric dye when possible, as powdered fabric dye must be mixed with hot water before it can be added to the soap.

Use the liquid dye sparingly, as too much dye will curdle your soap. For each 3/4-pound (340 g) batch of soap, 1/2 teaspoon (2.5 ml) of dye is usually sufficient. Add the dye just before your grated and remelted soap is ready to be poured into molds, and be sure to stir the dye in thoroughly. Different colors contain different amounts of sodium, so play it safe by adding no more than this and by performing a skin test with a finished dyed bar (see page 29).

Food dyes are perhaps the dyes least appropriate for the soap-maker's closet. Although they pose no health hazards, they do not hold up well over time, especially when they're exposed to light. If this limitation doesn't bother you and you don't have access to other types of dyes, by all means use food dyes.

LIQUID FABRIC DYES

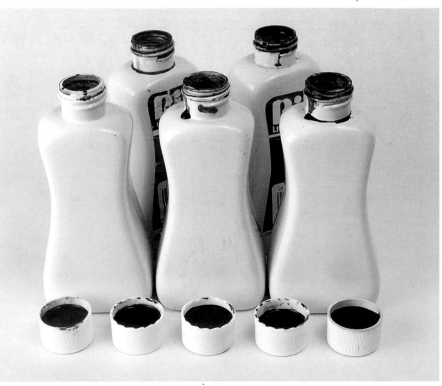

SOAPS DYED WITH NATURAL PIGMENTS

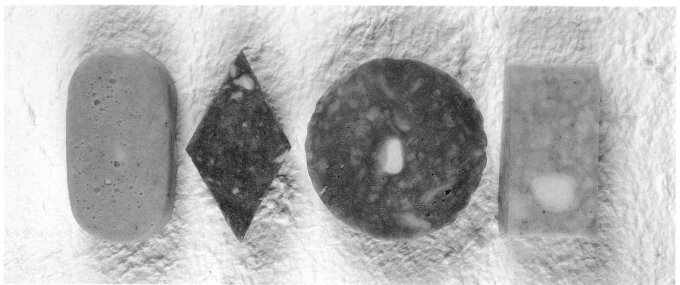

Pigments are natural dyes and offer another coloring option if you're opposed to using synthetic dyes in your soaps. They are made from ground rock and are used in certain types of paints. Available from pottery supply houses in powdered form and in a wide range of colors, pigments are easy to mix into milled and remelted soap. The pigments listed to the right are perfectly safe to use in soaps—with one exception: Never used pigment-dyed soaps on infants.

Because pigments vary widely in the intensity of their colors, it isn't possible to recommend an exact quantity to add to your soap, but I have found that 1 to 2 teaspoons (1.9 to 4 g) is usually sufficient to color a 12-ounce (340 g) batch. To prepare the pigment, mix it with just enough water to make a thin liquid. Then add the mixture to the remelted soap just as you would any other dye. If the shade that results isn't intense enough, you can always add more of the dissolved pigment.

EXAMPLES OF
NATURAL PIGMENTS

Suggested Pigments:

Brown ochre

Burnt umber

Green earth

Iron oxide

Prussian red

Raw umber

Red sienna

Ultramarine blue

Ultramarine purple

Ultramarine red

Yellow ochre

Yellow sienna

AMONG the earliest cleansing agents that people used were plants such as soapwort (*Saponaria officinalis*), the roots of which contain saponin. This natural substance produces suds when the roots are agitated in water.

SOAPS COLORED WITH
NATURAL DYES.

Natural dyes derived from plant materials are unfortunately more difficult to use, as the chemical makeup of soap affects them greatly. Although none of these natural dyes offers spectacular results, the two described here are relatively unaffected by soap and aren't terribly time-consuming to prepare or difficult to use.

TURMERIC (POWDERED)

Soap Color: Golden to orange

Preparation and Use: For each 3-pound (1.4 kg) batch of soap, use only 1 teaspoon (2 g) of this powerful dye, adding the powdered spice just before pouring the soap into the molds.

PAPRIKA (POWDERED)

Soap Color: Peach

Preparation and Use: Same as turmeric (opposite).

Substitutions

When you run out of a particular ingredient, especially fats, tallow, or oils, it's always tempting to substitute ingredients you have on hand. Doing so can be risky. Whenever you change the proportions or ingredients in a recipe, you're changing the character of the soap. Still, if the temptation proves irresistible, keep the following guidelines in mind:

■ Never make substitutions when preparing lye. Using any other substance will create a disaster.

■ Try to use a fat or oil with a similar consistency and character to the fat or oil you're replacing.

■ Don't change the required weights listed in the recipe. Use as much of the substitute ingredient as you would have of the original ingredient.

■ Keep the proportion of the fats and/or oils to the lye the same as the proportion called for in the original recipe.

■ Don't change the proportion of liquids to solids.

Chapter Three:
Working Carefully

The safety precautions and incidental information in this chapter are important and are here to save you from the sufferings of those who have gone before you. Read the entire chapter a couple of times before you attempt to make your first batch of soap.

LEARNING NEW HABITS

Several years ago, during a soap-making class that I was teaching, a student lamented, "There's so much to learn about soap making, and we haven't even started to make soap yet!" If you find yourself thinking similarly, relax. You're just experiencing what we've all had to go through at one time or another—learning a new discipline. Perhaps it's been awhile since you learned a new craft; if so, you might be experiencing a bit of rebelliousness, too! Everything that seems foreign to you now, however, will be old hat by the time you've made your third batch of soap, and once you've learned what you need to know, you won't soon forget it.

The rules presented here may seem harsh and difficult to retain, but if you follow them to the letter as you make your first soaps, they'll soon become habits and will give you the confidence to tackle each new project safely and enthusiastically. We're all creatures of habit; once you've learned good soap-making habits, they'll pay off for as long as you enjoy this craft.

SAFETY RULES

■ Protect your work station and the floor surrounding it by covering them with newspapers or other protective materials. Lye and liquid soap have a way of finding tabletops and floors when you're not prepared—so be prepared!

■ Make sure that the pitchers you select are safe for use with lye. Unless they're labeled "dishwasher safe," perform the following test. Place the pitchers upright in your sink and pour boiling water into them. Gently test the handles. The pitchers should not melt or become flexible, and the handles should not weaken at all. Fresh lye can reach temperatures of 170° to 200°F (77° to 93°C), so don't use pitchers that don't pass this test with flying colors.

■ Use your lye-mixing pitchers only for mixing lye. Using an indelible-ink pen, mark each pitcher clearly: "**LYE PITCHER! DO NOT USE FOR ANYTHING ELSE!**" Keep lye pitchers out of sight when they're not in use and keep them out of reach of children at all times. No one—repeat, no one—should be able to mistake them for beverage containers!

■ Read all safety precautions on the can of lye before you begin. If the granules or solution accidentally come in contact with your skin or eyes, flush immediately with cold water. If burns ensue, consult a physician. Even dry lye granules can burn your skin by attracting moisture from the air.

■ Always wear protective gloves and safety glasses or goggles while working with lye. Also wear them for clean-up; lye soap is caustic until it has cured thoroughly.

■ Lye can corrode metals, so remove all metal jewelry before making soap.

■ Never inhale lye fumes while you're mixing the lye with water, as the fumes may injure your lungs.

■ Place pitchers filled with hot lye solutions away from the edges of your work surface and out of reach of children and pets. Make sure the pitchers won't be in your way as you work.

■ Before you pour lye from a pitcher, make sure that the pitcher lid is tightly in place. Pour slowly and evenly to avoid splashing and the possible burns that might result.

■ When handling a pitcher of lye solution, always brace the bottom of the pitcher with one gloved hand as you grip the handle securely with the other.

■ Never leave fats and oils unattended while you're heating them. These substances are flammable and may catch fire if they're allowed to boil over. If you should ever have to deal with fats that have burst into flame inside the pot, first slide a tight-fitting lid across the top of the pot and then turn the burner off. (Do not bring the lid straight down onto the pot, or air currents will force the flames out and around to your hand.) The fire inside the pot will go out shortly after you've deprived it of oxygen in this fashion. Wait until the contents have cooled completely before attempting to remove the lid or move the pot. Also keep a good, all-purpose fire extinguisher in a convenient location and use it if necessary!

■ Store curing soaps well out of reach of animals and children. The lye in your basic soaps will remain caustic for several days after the bars are cut.

WEIGHING AND MEASURING

Every one of your soap ingredients must be carefully weighed. Doing this isn't difficult, but because mistakes can result in failed batches of soap, it's important to familiarize yourself with your scales and thermometers.

These instruments are all too easy to misread. Two common mistakes are glancing at the scale or thermometer too quickly and misjudging the weight or temperature that the gradation lines represent. Different manufacturers mark their products differently, so figure out what each line represents before you use these instruments.

Another common error is to assume that the ounces used to measure weight are equal to the ounce measurements of volume. Volume and weight are not the same! Unless otherwise specified, the recipes in this book refer to weight—not to volume. A conversion chart (see page 125), will prove helpful whether you use metric measurements or their U.S. equivalents. If you're short of an ingredient by just a small amount, see page 37 (for information on decreasing amounts in your selected recipe) and page 27 (for information on making substitutions).

ALLERGIES

Before using any handmade soap that includes scents, dyes, or additives, always perform a skin test to make sure that you aren't allergic to any of these ingredients. Apply the soap in normal fashion to the tender area on the inside of your upper arm. If you're sensitive to an ingredient in that soap, your skin will let you know, usually within eight hours.

If you plan to give away or sell your soaps, design small instruction cards which explain how to perform this test and include one with each bar or soap-filled basket.

Chapter Four:
Rendering Tallow

The first stage of the soap-making process is rendering. During this process, beef fat is melted in water in order to separate out any impurities in it. The purified fat which results is called tallow. As your family members may make painfully clear, rendering isn't the most pleasant part of soap making; the process tends to be messy, and the odors associated with it can be downright nasty, but unless you purchase tallow, rendering is unavoidable.

FROM FAT TO TALLOW

The higher the quality of your tallow, the better your soap will be. To make the highest-quality tallow, use beef suet, which, once rendered, makes an excellent soap base and a much harder soap than many other rendered fats. Although tallow rendered from ordinary beef fat trimmings can be used, it just doesn't measure up to suet-based tallow.

Unfortunately, suet isn't always easy to locate. At one time it could be found at any meat counter, but now that meat is processed at centralized locations, this isn't often the case. Spend some time calling grocery stores and butchers in your area.

Eventually, you'll find one that carries suet or that is willing to help you get it. You may be laughed at a few times. You may even be scolded. Persist until someone takes you seriously. Smaller shops and butchers are more likely to be helpful than large grocery stores.

If you're unable to find anything except ordinary beef fat or waste fats from the kitchen, then use them you must. The rendering process is the same, but your tallow will be softer, and the soap that you make with it won't be as hard or as high in quality as soap made with suet-based tallow.

When possible, make your tallow in large batches and freeze it until you need it. This method will limit your tallow-making activities to two or three times a year and will also ensure a more harmonious family life year round!

You may notice differences between one batch of tallow and the next, even when you use suet every time. I'm convinced that this has to do with the diet of the animal from which the suet has been taken, as well as with the animal's overall health. These differences shouldn't concern you; they're simply beyond your control.

INSTRUCTIONS FOR RENDERING

What You Need

- 3 to 5 pounds (1.4 to 2.3 kg) suet or other meat fat
- Water
- 2 to 4 tablespoons (17 to 34 g) salt
- Sharp knife
- Food processor with knife-blade attachment (optional)
- Large pot
- Long-handled wooden or plastic spoon
- Safety glasses or goggles
- Rubber or plastic gloves
- Wooden or stainless steel ladle
- Sieve or colander
- Primary mold

Method

1. In order to decrease the suet's melting time, you must increase its surface area by cutting or grinding it into the smallest pieces possible. The easiest way to do this is to have your local butcher or meat department grind the suet for you. For a slightly higher cost per pound or kilogram, you'll get suet that practically melts in the pot.

If this service isn't available to you, use a sharp knife to cut the suet into small pieces. If you have a food processor, use the knife-blade attachment to shred these pieces even finer. Be patient, though. Overloading your food processor will make a mess instead of saving time. (Avoid using a food processor to grind beef fat or waste kitchen fats; just cut up these ingredients by hand.)

2. Place the ground or freshly cut suet into a pot large enough to accommodate some expansion of the suet as it heats and bubbles. The suet should fill no more than half of the pot. Add 2 to 4 inches (5.1 to 10.2 cm) of water to the bottom of the pan. Also add the salt to help separate the impurities from the mixture.

3. Set the mixture over moderately high heat and put on your safety glasses and gloves. Stir the mixture gently as it heats up. The object is to get as much of the suet as possible to liquefy. Allow the mixture to come to a slow boil, watching it constantly, as it may ignite if it boils over. (If the mixture overheats, remove the pot from the heat and stir. Lower the heat and return the pot to it.) Mash the small pieces of suet with your spoon to release any trapped liquid fat and speed up the melting process, which will take at least 30 minutes for each 2 to 3 pounds (.9 to 1.4 kg) of suet and longer for larger amounts and bigger pieces. If the water begins to boil away, by all means add more, or the hot, diluted fat may sputter out of the pot. Be careful when adding water, as this may also cause some temporary sputtering.

4. When most of the suet has dissolved, remove the pot from the stove and allow the mixture to cool slightly. Then pour or ladle the mixture through a sieve (or, in a pinch, a colander), straining it into your primary mold. The sieve or colander will catch any debris: sinew, gristle, and meat.

5. Inspect the strained solids remaining in the sieve. If you've cooked the mixture long enough, these will be brown. Throw them away or mix them up with a little peanut butter and set them out for the birds. If you see large chunks of white fat mixed in with the strained solids, either return them to the pot with more water and salt, and repeat to render the remaining fat, or save them and add them to your next batch of suet.

6. Place the filled primary mold in your refrigerator overnight; you need not place the lid on the mold. As the mixture cools, the tallow will rise to the surface and solidify.

7. Remove the mold from the refrigerator and turn it upside down into your sink. Press the bottom of the mold to remove the block of tallow, allowing any liquid to drain away. (If most of the water boiled away during the melting stage, very little will remain in the mold.) If you started out with more ordinary fat than suet or if the fat contained much meat, you'll see a gelatin-like mass on the bottom of the block of tallow. Scrape this mass off and discard it.

8. You should now have a hard, firm, white or off-white block of tallow. Scrape away and discard any layers of debris on the block. Also scrape away any portions of the block that are soft or discolored. Sometimes the tallow will be speckled; as long as these speckles are in hard tallow, they can be tolerated. Refrigerate or freeze the tallow until you are ready to make your basic soap (see Chapter Five).

DURING Colonial times, tallow chandlers and soap boilers collected household fats and oils, and in return, they supplied each household with candles and finished soap.

Chapter Five:

Basic Soaps

Master instructions for making any basic soap are provided in this chapter and are followed by several basic soap recipes. Read the instructions first, select a recipe next, and then begin making your first batch of soap!

THE FIRST STEP

Whether you plan to make hand-cut bars of basic soap or hand-milled soaps, which can be sliced into bars or molded, the first part of the soap-making process is the same: You will make a batch of basic soap. In this process, hot lye and melted fats and/or oils are brought to equal temperatures, mixed together, poured into a primary mold, and cured.

To make hand-milled soaps, you'll grate, remelt, and mold (or slice) the batch of basic soap, mixing in fragrances, colors, and additives during the remelting stage. Although ingredients such as scent oils may be added to basic soaps, they're usually mixed in during the hand-milling process instead. If you'd like to add scent oil to a basic soap, do so just before the soap is poured into the primary mold; stir well to disperse the scent evenly.

MASTER INSTRUCTIONS FOR BASIC SOAPS

TIPS

▪ The trickiest part of this procedure is equalizing the temperatures of the lye solution and of the melted fats and/or oils at 100°F (38°C) before they are mixed together. Juggling the temperatures until they match one another can be done in several ways. The lye solution, which heats up tremendously as it's mixed, can be left to cool gradually as you heat the fats and/or oils, can be cooled more rapidly in a cold-water bath, or can be made several hours in advance (or even the night before) and then rewarmed in a hot-water bath. See Step 8 for details.

▪ For the sake of brevity, the following instructions use the term "fat" to describe fats and/or oils. The basic soap recipe that you select will specify which fats and/or oils to use.

What You Need

- Ingredients for selected basic soap recipe (see pages 38-45)
- Newspapers
- Safety glasses or goggles
- Rubber or plastic gloves
- Scale
- 2 lye pitchers
- Long-handled wooden or plastic spoon
- 2 kitchen thermometers
- Large dishwater pan
- Soap pot
- Wooden or stainless steel ladle
- Primary mold with lid
- Insulating materials
- Freezer or butcher paper; sheet of rigid plastic; or needlepoint screen
- Flexible cardboard for making templates
- Ruler
- Pencil
- Scissors
- Sharp knife
- Nut pick or other pointed tool
- Vegetable peeler or paring knife

Method

1. Read through all the steps carefully. Then select a basic soap recipe. Cover a large, flat counter top or table and the surrounding floor with several layers of newspapers. Assemble your equipment and ingredients, and make sure that all the equipment meets the requirements described in Chapter One.

2. Reread the safety precautions in Chapter Three. Then put on your gloves and safety glasses!

3. Weigh the required amount of lye into one of the pitchers. To do this, use either of the following methods:

METHOD #1 Place the empty pitcher on the scale and set the scale at zero. Then use the pitcher as a weighing container. If you've set the scale correctly, it will register the weight of the lye but not the weight of the pitcher.

METHOD #2 Set the scale at zero and weigh the pitcher. Then calculate the weight of the pitcher plus the weight of the required lye. Add lye to the pitcher until you reach this total weight.

Set the pitcher of lye aside.

4. Using the same method that you used to weigh the lye, weigh the required amount of water in the empty pitcher. (Be careful not to place the water in the pitcher that contains lye!)

5. Make sure that the pitcher with lye in it is resting on a protected surface. Carefully lift the pitcher with water in it, and pour the water into the pitcher containing lye. For safety's sake, you must avoid splashing! Don't make the mistake of adding the lye to the water.

6. After you've added all the water to the lye, stir the solution gently with a wooden spoon until you're sure that all the lye has dissolved. If you don't stir thoroughly, the lye may cake on the bottom of the pitcher and will be difficult to break up and dissolve. Place one of your thermometers in the pitcher. The lye, which will have heated up considerably, is likely to register from 150° to 200°F (66° to 93°C).

7. If you don't plan to make soap for several hours or more, just set the pitcher of hot lye solution aside to cool in a safe place, placing it on sheets of newspaper or an old towel. Be sure the lid to the pitcher is firmly in place.

8. Before continuing, read this step and Step 9 carefully, as you will be working on these steps simultaneously.

At this stage, you should either have a cool lye solution, made well in advance, or a hot lye solution that has just been mixed. As you melt the fats and then cool them to 100°F (see Steps 9 through 12), you must bring the temperature of the lye to 100°F (38°C), too.

To rewarm cool lye, place the pitcher, with the lid removed and a thermometer in place, in a pan of hot tap water. Watch the lye temperature closely so that you don't overheat the solution. If you accidentally let the solution get too warm, remove the pitcher from the pan and allow it to cool down again.

To cool down a batch of hot lye solution, fill a pan or your sink with cold water. Place the pitcher of lye in it, making sure that there isn't so much water in the bath that the pitcher floats; if the pitcher tips, the lye may burn you. You'll also have to start all over again! Place a thermometer in the solution and stir the solution gently with your spoon, monitoring the temperature carefully.

As the temperature approaches 100°F, remove the lye pitcher from the cold or warm bath.

9. As you continue to monitor and adjust the temperature of the lye solution, weigh out the required fats for your selected recipe. If your scale will measure up to 25 pounds (11.4 kg) and can be reset at zero, weigh the

ingredients in the soap pot itself, setting the scale back to zero before adding each one. With smaller scales, it's better to weigh the ingredients separately and then place them in the pot one by one. Be precise no matter which method you choose; even small mistakes can result in failed batches of soap.

10. Once the fats have been measured and placed in the soap pot, set the pot over low to medium heat and stir the contents gently to help them melt. Use your mixing spoon to mash any small floating pieces. (Don't worry about tiny pieces.) Heat the mixture just to the point at which the fats have melted, then remove the pot from the stove.

11. To cool off the fats quickly, place the soap pot in a cold-water bath in your sink, but make sure that the water isn't frigid, or the fats may begin to solidify again on the inner surfaces of the pot. Stir continuously to help reduce the temperature, and as it approaches 105°F (41°C), remove the pot from the cold-water bath.

12. Continue to juggle the temperatures of the lye solution and the fats so that they both reach 100°F simultaneously. This may be frustrating at first, but after you've made a few successful batches of soap, you'll learn that patience has its rewards! Keep your head, always use care (especially when handling the lye), and don't panic. Just continue to use the cold and warm baths.

Occasionally, you may find that the fats solidify slightly as they approach the target temperature. This is especially likely to happen with recipes that call for tallow and/or coconut oil. Double-check your thermometer against another thermometer; if it's accurate, ignore this slight solidification and continue. If the thermometer isn't accurate or if the fats solidify completely, remelt the fats just to the melting point in a warm-water bath and recheck the temperature with a different thermometer.

13. Double-check the temperatures of both the lye solution and the melted fats, making sure that they're both between 95° and 100°F (35° to 38°C).

14. Be sure that you're wearing your rubber gloves and safety glasses and that your work surface is protected. Tighten the lid securely onto your lye pitcher; the lid must not come off during the pouring process. Then, while stirring the fats gently and steadily,

pour the lye solution into the soap pot in a thin, steady stream, stirring the mixture continuously as you do so. Only by stirring in this fashion can you be certain that all of the lye will be absorbed into the fats. If you see substantial amounts of lye floating on top of the fats, stop adding more until you've stirred in the floating lye. Then resume pouring and stirring until all the lye has been absorbed.

15. Continue to stir the mixture gently. The fats must be kept in smooth motion at all times. Be careful; stirring haphazardly can result in dangerous spilling or splashing of the caustic solution. As you continue to stir, the mixture will thicken, turn opaque, and become grainy rather than smooth.

Keep stirring until you can see what are known as *trailings*; these are lines of soap that float on the surface of, yet remain distinct from, the soap in the pot (see the photo below). Trailings look a bit like the ripples on top of instant pudding, although at times they're much more subtle in appearance. The best way to test for them is to lift your spoon out of the mixture and drizzle a thread of soap across the surface of the soap in the pot. Just how distinct the trailings are depends largely on how thick the soap has become.

Trailings don't jump up and down to catch your attention—more's the pity—and can be hard to identify, especially for beginners. Poor lighting and particular angles of vision make them especially difficult to see.

The stirring process can last anywhere from fifteen minutes to one hour, depending on the ingredients in the soap you're making. Soaps that are high in tallow, for example, will show trailings much more easily than soaps containing large proportions of liquid vegetable oils. If you've stirred for nearly an hour and still can't see trailings, go ahead and proceed as if you have seen them. The signs are probably there, but you're not experienced enough yet to recognize what you're seeing.

Your soap should still be warm when you stop stirring it. Although it's possible to stir too long, your common sense should kick in before this happens. Once you've made several batches of soap, your experience and instincts will tell you when to stop stirring.

16. Gently pour or ladle the warm soap into the primary mold. Scrape the sides of the pot and add the scrapings to the mold, too.

17. Place the lid on the mold and wrap the entire mold in insulating materials. Take this step as quickly as possible, or your soap will "catch cold."

18. Place the wrapped mold in a warm place and allow it to sit undisturbed for 48 hours. The soap must cool slowly. As it does, it will begin to "set up" or harden inside the mold. Cooling the soap too rapidly will ruin it by causing separations, either partial or complete, of the lye and fats.

19. After 48 hours have passed, unwrap the primary mold and remove the lid. Unless the surrounding air is especially cold, your soap should still be warm to the touch. (Note that the soap is still caustic, so touch it only while wearing gloves!) The soap will

look solid, but your gloved finger should leave an impression on its surface. Inspect the soap by looking through the sides and bottom of the clear primary mold; all surfaces of the block of soap should appear solid. If you see a layer of liquid or any liquid bubbles, or if the soap looks separated, curdled, or abnormal in any way, refer to Chapter Nine, "Troubleshooting and Adjustments," before continuing.

20. If the surface of the soap is still very soft, leave the soap in the uncovered mold and expose it to the air for a day or two; the surface should harden as the soap begins to dry. When the exposed surface is finger-impression hard, gently pull the sides of the mold away from the sides of the soap.

Then turn the mold upside down over a sink or tub and press the bottom of the mold to release the soap. (Avoid working over a tabletop; trapped lye in the soap will damage the table and may burn you as well.)

Be especially careful with the block of soap if you plan to make hand-cut bars; you'll want as perfect a block as possible. If the block doesn't release easily, give it more time to dry; especially soft soaps may take up to several more days.

21. Place the block of soap on a clean surface; white freezer or butcher paper, a rigid sheet of plastic, or a plastic needlepoint screen will all work well. Don't use cardboard or newsprint, as the soap will still be soft enough to absorb colors from these materials.

At this point, you'll need to decide whether to slice the block into bars of basic soap or take the additional steps required to turn the block of basic soap into hand-milled soap. Your choice will depend on what your ultimate expectations are for your finished product, how much time you have to devote to it, and how much experimenting you're willing to do with additives. Either method will leave you with a beautiful and useful product. If you decide to make hand-cut bars of basic soap, just move on to Step 22. If you'd rather hand-mill your soap, turn now to Chapter Six.

22. Check the block of soap every day; when it's as hard as Swiss cheese—a process that should take a week or less—it's dry enough to be scored and cut into bars. Don't let the block get too hard to slice with a knife.

23. Select dimensions for your finished bars of basic soap. Standard rectangular bars are approximately 3 inches wide by 4 inches long (7.6 by 10.2 cm), but because the cut bars will shrink as they dry, you'll need to add 1/2 inch (1.3 cm) to each dimension.

24. To mark the block of soap for cutting, you'll need two flexible cutting templates. The cardboard from empty cereal boxes makes an ideal material for these. Measure and cut one template as long as the large block of soap and as wide as you'd like your cut bars to be—3-1/2 inches (8.9 cm), for example. Make the other template as wide as the large block of soap and as long as the desired bars—4-1/2 inches (11.4 cm), for example.

25. Lay the longer template along the length of the large block and, using a nut pick or similar instrument,

score the upper face of the block along the length of the template. Move the template so that one long edge rests along the line you've just scored. Then score along the template's opposite edge. Continue to score as many rows as possible along the large block.

26. Lay the shorter template across the block's width and use it in similar fashion to score a series of lines across the block's upper surface. When you're finished, you'll have marked a grid of rectangles onto the large block.

27. Heat the blade of a sharp knife by submerging it in hot water and use the warmed blade to cut along the longer scored lines. Make sure not to tilt the knife as you cut, or your bars will have sloped edges! Then cut along the shorter lines to form the individual bars. (Keep all cutting scraps and use them to make the Soap Balls described on pages 108-109.)

28. The hand cut bars of basic soap must now cure—the last stage of saponification. As they do, they'll become less caustic, somewhat lighter in weight, and smaller. Place the bars on plastic needlepoint mesh, white paper, or rigid plastic; they will still contain moisture and may pick up colors from other materials. Space them evenly and don't allow them to touch each other.

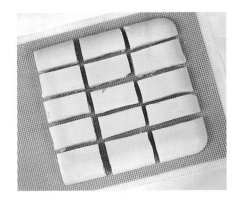

29. Allow the bars to dry for about two weeks or until the surfaces are very hard to the touch. The best way to test whether or not your soap is ready is to wash your hands with it. You'll probably have small, unnoticeable breaks in your skin, and if the soap isn't ready, the lye in it will tell you right away by making your skin sting!

Don't be surprised if shrinkage causes the edges of the bars to become warped and uneven. This shrinkage is inevitable, but you can minimize its effects by turning the bars over once the upper surfaces have hardened. For instructions on removing surface irregularities and other blemishes, and for tips on storing and wrapping your bars of soap, refer to Chapters Nine and Ten.

Doubling and Halving Recipes

As long as your math skills are up to snuff, go right ahead and double or triple recipes. Don't try to make batches any larger, however; huge batches are just too awkward to pour into a primary mold, and ladling them into the mold is too time consuming and messy.

Decreasing recipes is not only possible, but can be downright helpful when you're short on ingredients or when you want to conduct an experiment such as using a new oil for the first time. Do keep in mind that smaller volumes of soap cool faster than larger volumes and that when soap cools too quickly, the lyes and fats tend to separate. For this reason, don't work with batches smaller than one-quarter of a recipe. You'll need a postal scale, as you'll be measuring fairly small increments in any reduced recipe.

BASIC SOAP RECIPES

The big surprise to these basic soap recipes is that even though their ingredients are so similar (tallow and/or oils, lye, and water), the soaps they yield are entirely different from one another. Select your personal favorites and slice them into hearty hand-cut bars for everyday use, or transform them into the hand-milled soaps described in Chapters Six and Seven.

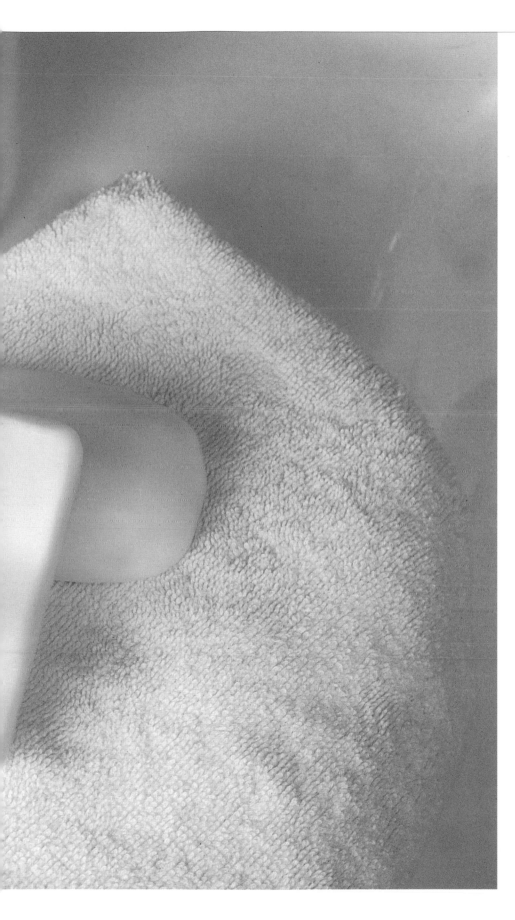

PLAIN WHITE SOAP

This is a multifaceted soap, good for making hand-cut bars of basic soap and for milling.

Characteristics

- White or off-white in color
- Mild
- Long-lasting, small creamy bubbles
- Shows trailings quickly
- Sets up and dries quickly
- May be milled and remelted in either moist or dry state
- Shows detailing well; best soap for fancy molds
- Accepts additives very well
- Quite hard when cured

Ingredients

- 32 ounces blended vegetable oil or olive oil
- 74 ounces tallow
- 3 ounces cocoa butter
- 14 ounces lye
- 41 ounces cold water

VEGETARIAN'S CHOICE SOAP

For folks who would prefer to avoid animal-based cleansing products, here's a very basic but effective soap.

Characteristics

- White or off-white in color
- Extremely mild
- Lathers quite well
- Takes longer than most to show trailings
- Slower to set up and dry than most soaps
- Must be milled and remelted when moist
- Mills and molds well, but is best suited to larger, more open molds
- Accepts additives well
- Always a relatively soft soap, but using olive oil makes it somewhat harder

Ingredients

- 42 ounces blended vegetable oil or olive oil
- 30 ounces coconut oil
- 28 ounces vegetable shortening
- 6 ounces cocoa butter
- 3 ounces castor oil
- 14 ounces lye
- 41 ounces cold water

PALM OIL SOAP

Very rich, mild, and creamy, this is a wonderful facial soap. It's also a favorite for people whose skin is sensitive or dry.

Characteristics

- Color will vary. Salmon to orange if you use red palm oil; white if you use bleached palm oil
- Very mild
- Lathers luxuriantly; small, long-lasting bubbles
- Shows trailings readily
- Sets up readily; dries fairly slowly, never to the crisp feel of many soaps
- Must be milled and remelted while moist
- Mills and molds well, but is better suited to larger, open molds
- Accepts additives moderately well
- Will feel outwardly dry but will be somewhat sticky even after the milling and drying process

Ingredients

- 56 ounces tallow
- 22 ounces palm oil
- 28 ounces olive oil
- 15 ounces lye
- 41 ounces cold water

COCOA CREME SOAP

Because it includes coconut oil, this soap isn't quite as mild as the others described in this chapter. The difference will only matter to those with sensitive skins.

Characteristics

- Creamy white in color
- Slightly harsh
- Lathers readily; large, creamy bubbles
- Shows trailings relatively quickly
- Moderately quick to set up, but dries slowly. Will eventually feel outwardly dry, but will never have the crisp feel of other soaps
- Must be milled and remelted when moist
- Mills and molds well, but is best suited to larger, open molds
- Accepts additives well
- Moderately hard when thoroughly cured

Ingredients

- 44 ounces tallow
- 30 ounces coconut oil
- 30 ounces blended vegetable oil or olive oil
- 6 ounces cocoa butter
- 14 ounces lye
- 41 ounces cold water

NINETEENTH-CENTURY SOAP

The following ingredients make up an old-fashioned soap that is nevertheless very mild.

Characteristics
- Clean white in color
- Very mild
- Lathers well; small, creamy bubbles
- Shows trailings quickly
- Sets up quickly and dries readily
- Must be milled and remelted when moist
- Mills and molds well; acceptable for very fancy molds
- Accepts additives well
- Hard when cured

Ingredients
- 44 ounces tallow
- 30 ounces olive oil
- 28 ounces lard
- 14 ounces lye
- 41 ounces cold water

HOMESTEADER'S SOAP

The nature of this coarse but mild soap will depend largely on the nature of the fat you use. In fact, you'll be as unable to predict final results as the pioneers were! If this uncertainty appeals to you, go ahead and experiment. If it doesn't, restrict yourself to suet-based tallow. If you use kitchen fats, you'll need to scent this soap in order to avoid unpleasant odors later (see Chapters Two and Six).

Characteristics
- Off-white in color
- Quite mild
- Moderately creamy bubbles
- Shows trailings quickly
- Sets up quickly and dries readily
- May be milled and remelted when moist or dry
- Mills and molds well; suitable for all but the smallest of molds
  Soap Balls (see pages 108-109) or hand-cut bars also recommended
- Accepts additives well
- Quite hard, unless chicken fat used

Ingredients
- 106 ounces rendered waste fat or tallow, or a combination of both
- 14 ounces lye
- 41 ounces cold water

UNTIL the early 1900s, making soap in North American households was a task that fell to women, who saved and stored cooking fats and oils and who usually made soap only once a year.

OLIVE OIL CASTILE SOAP

A traditional recipe from Castile, Spain, this makes a beautiful and very mild soap.

Characteristics

- Off-white in color
- Exceptionally mild
- Lathers quickly; plenty of medium-size, creamy bubbles
- Trailings difficult to see
- Sets up quickly and dries quickly
- May be milled and remelted when moist or dry
- Mills and molds very well; well suited for all molds
- Accepts additives well
- Very hard and long-lasting

Ingredients

- 52 ounces olive oil
- 7 ounces lye
- 20 ounces cold water

SPECIAL INSTRUCTIONS FOR OLIVE OIL CASTILE SOAP

This soap is made by following Steps 1 through 17 of the master instructions, but because the recipe includes only liquid oils, the wrapped primary mold must be checked twice a day. To do this, carefully unwrap the mold and uncover the soap. You are likely to notice a thin layer of oil on top. Using your wooden spoon, carefully stir this layer of oil back into the soap, then replace the lid and rewrap the mold. Repeat this process once every 12 hours or so until the layer of oil no longer forms. Then proceed as usual.

Chapter Six:
Hand-Milled Soaps

At some point in history—no one is sure when or where—a soap maker discovered that when basic soaps went through the modified cooking process now known as milling, the soaps were greatly improved.

THE ADVANTAGES OF HAND-MILLED SOAPS

Today, you'll almost always see milled (also known as French-milled) facial, toilet, and bath soaps prominently displayed among other soaps in the cosmetic aisles of your favorite stores. Soap companies never miss an opportunity to advertise the fact that their soaps are milled; they know that this adds value to their product!

Hand-milled soaps have a more pleasing texture than soaps which haven't been milled. They last longer, too—an especially important factor when you consider that handmade basic soaps are considerably softer than the soaps you purchase at stores. Milling your soaps also allows you to use scents, colors, and additives to their best advantage. When these are added as basic soaps are being made, the caustic lye in the liquid soap often damages them. When you make hand-milled bars, on the other hand, these extra ingredients are mixed in at a stage at which lye is no longer present. In addition, the milling process permits you to mold your soaps in as sophisticated a manner as you choose.

SELECTING RECIPES

To create milled soap, you must first select a hand-milled soap recipe from Chapter Seven. You will also need to select a basic soap recipe and make a large block of basic soap (see Chapter Five). Keep the following considerations in mind as you choose your hand-milled and basic soap recipes:

■ If you plan to use fancy molds for your milled soap, be sure to choose a basic soap that is easily poured after milling.

■ Your selected basic soap recipe must be compatible with the type of milled soap you are trying to make. Don't use a harsh basic soap recipe, for example, when making a milled soap such as skin-softening Calendula Soap (see page 63).

■ A few hand-milled soap recipes call for additives (buttermilk is one) which soften soaps and should therefore be used only in conjunction with recipes for the harder basic soaps. Refer to Chapter Two for descriptions of all ingredients.

■ Some of the basic soap recipes in this book yield soaps that can be milled more readily than others. To find out which basic soap recipes are best for milling, just refer to the descriptions given for each one in Chapter Five.

■ As the lists on the following page indicate, some basic soaps can be grated and remelted when they are either moist or dry. Others, however, must be milled while they are still relatively moist in order to make sure that they will melt to the correct consistency. If you overdry these basic soaps, you won't be able to pour them into the molds once they're milled. Instead, they'll chase your mixing spoon around the melting pot and become a large, unmanageable mess. Do not despair if this happens! You can still use large molds, packing the soap in as best you can, or you can make Floating Soap (see page 111) or Soap Balls (see pages 108-109).

Soaps that should be milled while moist should be grated as soon as they're the consistency of soft cheese. Although it's best to remelt these grated soaps as soon as possible, you may store them in airtight containers for up to one week before doing so. Refrigerate the containers to prevent the growth of mildews or molds. Soaps that can be milled either moist or dry may be grated at your convenience and, after they're dry, stored indefinitely in jars or plastic containers until you're ready to remelt them.

MASTER INSTRUCTIONS FOR HAND-MILLED SOAPS

As you follow these instructions, keep in mind that they are general in nature. Specific information on scents, colors, and additives is provided in the individual recipes for milled soaps.

TIPS

■ Unless your selected hand-milled soap recipe specifies otherwise, always add scents, dyes, and additives just before the remelted soap is poured into the molds.

■ Heavier additives (sand, pumice, oatmeal, honey, bran, coffee, and corn-meal, for example) will sink to the bottom of the mold if they're added when the melted soap is still hot and thin in consistency. If you do mix in your additives too soon, when steam is still rising from the top of the soap, let the soap cool. Then stir it again to redistribute the additives before pouring the soap into the molds. You may also reheat and remold bars in which additives have sunk to the bottom.

■ No one can tell you exactly how much fragrance you will need to include in a soap, so specific quantities aren't provided in the hand-milled soap recipes. Because oils differ in strength (essential oils differ from synthetic oils in this respect) and because personal tastes vary widely, your nose will be the best guide. Even for the less robust fragrances, you should need to purchase no more than 1/2 to 1 ounce (14.2 to 28.4 g) of oil per 3/4 pound (340 g) of soap. As long as you're going to the expense of purchasing these oils, do add enough fragrance to ensure that your soaps are still attractively scented in several months' time. Some of the fragrance will dissipate, so you'll want to overscent the soap slightly when you make it.

■ When adding liquefied fruit or vegetables, which should be incorporated just before you pour the soap, deduct the amount of water that you added to the blender from the water called for in the hand-milled soap recipe. If you forget to do this, the resulting soap is likely to be too soft and will shrink a great deal. To prevent the fresh ingredients in these soaps from mildewing, provide excellent air circulation for the drying bars and turn them frequently as they cure. Also be sure to perform a skin-allergen test (see page 29) with soaps made in this fashion.

■ Dyes differ widely, so follow the general instructions that come with the type you buy. In general, dyes should be added at the same time that fragrances are added, just before pouring the remelted soap into individual molds.

■ To ensure consistent color throughout each batch of milled soap, make sure that all small soap particles have melted before adding dyes, which won't be absorbed into undissolved lumps of soap. If you find that you're unable to make a perfectly smooth soap, don't worry. Simply allow one-third to one-half of the soap bits to remain unmelted, then add the dye, following the instructions that come with it, and pour the soap into the molds. The resulting soap will be attractively speckled!

What You Need

- At least 12 ounces (340 g) of any basic soap (see Chapter Five)
- Ingredients for selected hand-milled soap recipe
- Sharp knife
- Hand-held kitchen grater
- Airtight plastic storage containers
- Stainless steel, enamel, or glass saucepan, 2 to 3 quart (1.9 to 2.8 l) capacity
- Wooden spoon
- Soap molds
- Rubber spatula
- Plastic needlepoint screen, cardboard box lids, white freezer paper, or butcher paper

Method

1. One to seven days after removing the block of basic soap from the primary mold, the soap will be hard enough to cut into chunks and grated. Exactly how long this hardening process will take depends on several factors, including the type of basic soap you've made (recipes vary in degrees of final soap hardness), the air temperature, and the humidity.

2. When the block of basic soap has dried sufficiently, use a sharp knife to cut it into rectangular or square chunks that will be easy to grip as you grate them. Wear your gloves as you do this; the soap may still be caustic to the touch!

3. Using a hand-held kitchen grater—not a blender or food processor—grate the soap into small pieces. Work over an air-tight container (with the lid removed, of course), letting the pieces drop into it. When you're working with softer soaps such as Palm Oil Soap, you may find that the slicing surface of the grater is easier to use than the surfaces with holes in them.

If the soap is so soft that it compresses under the pressure of grating or yields drops of liquid, stop! Your soap needs just a bit more drying time. To speed up the process and save your arms, spread the grating step out over a couple of days. Grate the outer surfaces of each chunk, setting the softer inner portions aside to dry a bit longer and grating these as they become a bit harder.

Making Larger Batches of Hand-Milled Soaps

Depending on the number of molds you have, you may want to increase the amounts of basic soap and water that you use when you make milled soaps. If you choose to increase your recipe, use the chart provided here to calculate proportions of soap and water. Don't forget that you'll also need to increase the amounts of additives called for in the hand-milled soap recipe you've selected. The hand-milled soap recipes in the next chapter are all based on the use of 12 ounces (340 g) of soap and 9 ounces (255 g) of water, so be sure to calculate the percentage by which you're increasing your recipe, and make adjustments accordingly.

Grated Soap	Water
3/4 pound (340 g)	9 ounces (255 g)
1 pound (453 g)	12 ounces (340 g)
1-1/2 pounds (680 g)	18 ounces (510 g)
2 pounds (907 g)	24 ounces (680 g)
3 pounds (1.4 kg)	36 ounces (1 kg)

4. When you're ready to start the remelting process, place 12 ounces (341 g) of grated soap and 9 ounces (255 g) of water in a stainless steel, glass, or enamel saucepan. This saucepan should be substantially smaller than your soap pot because the grated soap will heat too quickly—and may even scorch—in a pot that is too large.

5. Using a wooden spoon, gently stir the grated soap and water, stirring just enough to mix them together. Then place the saucepan over medium-low heat. Your goal is not to boil the soap but to heat it very gradually.

Don't stir the heating soap continuously, as doing so will create too many suds; you don't want to end up with a thick layer of bubbles on top of the liquid soap when you pour it. Stir just often enough to make sure that the soap isn't sticking to the bottom of the pan. Allow the bottom layer to heat up, stir it gently to disperse it throughout the saucepan, and then allow the new bottom layer to heat up again, repeating until all the soap has been warmed and has melted. You may need to add a bit of water now and then.

6. Continue to stir periodically until the soap has liquefied completely. Depending on the basic soap with which you're working and whether or not you have increased the size of the recipe (see page 49), this may take from twenty minutes to one hour. If you're making a plain soap for household use, a few random lumps of unmelted soap aren't worth worrying about, but if you're making filled, colored, or scented soaps, the melted soap must be smooth so that the additives will be evenly distributed.

Some of the basic soaps, such as Vegetarian's Choice and Cocoa Creme, will tend to form a very thick paste before they liquefy. Be patient. It may take up to an hour for one of these soaps to cooperate. (If you find yourself with a soap that just won't melt, you can turn it into Floating Soap or Soap Balls!)

7. When the soap has liquefied, remove it from the heat and stir it gently as it cools. If the soap is too hot when it's poured, it will shrink a great deal in the molds, and because fancy molds tend to be small anyway, the resulting bars will be very small indeed.

Experienced soap makers can tell by sight when the soap is ready to be poured. Beginners should aim for a soap temperature of 150° to 160°F (66° to 71°C). Keep in mind that thickening additives such as oatmeal may necessitate pouring at higher temperatures. If, after 15 minutes of stirring, the soap shows no signs of shrinkage in the saucepan, it won't shrink in the molds.

8. Just before pouring the soap, mix in the additives, scents, and/or fragrances specified in your selected hand-milled soap recipe. Stir the mixture thoroughly to disperse the ingredients well.

9. Pour or ladle the cooled soap into the individual molds. If the soap has thickened significantly, tap each filled mold on your work surface so that any air pockets will be filled with soap. Fill each mold as completely as possible, but avoid letting soap spill over the sides as this will affect the look of the finished bar, will make removal from the molds difficult, and is also wasteful! Use a rubber spat-

ula to smooth off the soap at the top of the mold and to scrape the very last bit from the spoon.

Note that greasing your molds isn't usually necessary and can cause a buildup of sticky gum on their inner surfaces. If, after you've gained some experience, you decide that a particular mold does need greasing, use any type of vegetable oil and be sure to wash the mold thoroughly after use.

10. Allow the surface of the soap in each mold to skim over, then place the molds in the freezer. (Although freezing the molds isn't absolutely necessary, it does make removing the bars much easier.) If your freezer space is limited, you may stack the molds or freeze them in shifts.

11. When the bars have frozen solid, which will take anywhere from 1-1/2 to several hours, remove them from the molds; you may need to give each mold a gentle squeeze to do this. If squeezing doesn't help, tap the mold gently in one hand, on a table, or on a counter top. Allowing the molds to thaw slightly or running hot water over their backs will also help to release the soaps. The milled soaps will still be slightly soft; handle them carefully in order not to mar them.

Two-Piece Molds

Three-dimensional shaped soaps are made with two-piece molds. To use these molds to their best advantage, pour and freeze each individual half, and remove the halves from the molds. Next, reheat a little of the soft soap remaining in your saucepan, and spread this liberally across one half's flat surface. Press the halves firmly together. As the "glue" dries, you may need to fill in the seams by pressing a bit more soft soap into them.

12. Your molded soaps are now ready for a final drying. After removing the soaps from the molds, place them on plastic needlepoint screen. To increase air circulation under the screen, staple the screen across an old window frame. White paper will make an adequate substitute for this screen. Place the soaps in a protected area where they won't be disturbed.

The bars are sufficiently cured when they're hard to the touch and when they don't give under pressure from your fingertips. The length of this curing time will depend on the basic recipe ingredients, the drying conditions, and the additives you have used. Curing may take from two weeks to a month—or even longer for extra large molds.

13. Check the bars about one week after they've been unmolded. You may notice that they've warped slightly. This will be particularly noticeable with rectangular bars or bars with long edges and will become accentuated with further drying. To combat this warping, check to see that the upper surface has hardened and then turn the bars over. You may need to turn the bars several times depending on the molds you've used. Some bars, such as those made in the gelatin molds pictured on pages 14-15, may never need turning.

Soaps containing fresh additives (goat's milk, milk and honey, or flower petals, for example) will need to be watched carefully during the drying process, as they will sometimes develop mold if they're aren't dried quickly enough. Choose a warm, dry location, turn the bars often, and make sure that they have good air circulation. (Elevating these bars so that air can circulate underneath them will help.) Plastic mesh is an ideal drying surface for bars of this type.

14. The last steps—finishing, storing, and wrapping your soaps—are described in Chapter Ten.

Congratulations! You've worked long and hard to reach this point. Why not reward yourself by taking a relaxing bath—with some of your hand-milled soap?

During both World Wars I and II, natural fats and oils were scarce and expensive. The need for soap, however, increased dramatically due to the military's huge need for cleaning agents. A less expensive and more plentiful alternative to natural fats and oils was discovered in petroleum oil, which was used to fuel aircraft during war time. From this oil, detergents were developed.

The new detergents differed from soaps in one important respect; they worked better in hard water. Before water softeners existed, and when soap was still made at home, clothing often turned grey with time because soap curds deposited on the fabric couldn't be completely rinsed off in hard water. Detergents were a blessing to people with "dishwater grey" clothes.

Chapter Seven:
Hand-Milled Soap Recipes

Any basic soap can be transformed into several different hand-milled soaps by grating it, remelting it, and incorporating different fragrances, colors, and additives. Once you've tried a few of the hand-milled soap recipes provided in this chapter, you'll soon be custom designing soaps for special friends—and for special occasions. By all means experiment. Revel in the sheer number of possibilities!

USING THE RECIPES

The recipes in this chapter are designed to be used in conjunction with the "Master Instructions for Hand-Milled Soaps" in Chapter Six. To make hand-milled soap, first select one of the recipes in this chapter. As you'll note, each of these recipes comes with specific instructions. Next, turn back to the master instructions in Chapter Six. Follow these master instructions, adding your hand-milled soap ingredients as directed in the recipe you've selected.

As you use these recipes, keep several important facts in mind:

■ Every recipe is formulated for use with 12 ounces (340 g) of grated basic soap and 9 ounces (255 g) of water. For information on increasing or decreasing the size of the batch you make, turn to page 37.

■ The fragrance and color suggestions included in these recipes are just that—suggestions! Because dyes and fragrances vary in their strengths, exact amounts are not provided. Let your personal taste and your access to particular fragrances and dyes be your guides. For more information on the use of these substances, turn to pages 24-27 and 48.

■ When a recipe calls for several drops of fragrance, you may use either essential oils or synthetic fragrance oils.

■ Most of the ingredients listed in these recipes should be added just before the soap is ready to pour into molds. Exceptions are noted in the recipe instructions.

Abrasive Soaps

Abrasive soaps remove dead outer layers of skin and expose the fresh layers underneath. Their degree of abrasiveness depends on the type and quantity of additive used. Sand, for example, makes a great hand cleaner for gardeners, but even gardeners wouldn't want to use it on their faces!

ALMOND MEAL SOAP

This soap is an excellent body or face scrub. The sweet almond oil in it is soothing to the skin.

Ingredients

- 1 to 2 cups (152 to 304 g) unshelled almonds
- 3 teaspoons (15 ml) sweet almond oil
- Several drops of sandalwood fragrance

Method

Place the almonds in a saucepan with just enough water to cover. Simmer for five minutes. Drain and cool by running cold water over them. Remove the skins. Grind the nuts in a blender until fine. Melt the basic soap and water in a saucepan. Add the almond meal and oil and stir until slightly thickened. Scent lightly and pour into molds.

GARDENER'S FRIEND SOAP

An excellent cleanser for people who work with their hands, this soap should be used on the hands only, as it is very abrasive.

Ingredients

- 1/4 cup (.24 l) lemon juice
- 1/2 to 3/4 cup (177 to 265 g) clean sand
- 1/4 to 1/2 cup (73 to 145 g) finely ground pumice

Method

Melt the basic soap and water together in a saucepan, substituting the lemon juice for 1/4 cup (.24 l) of the water. Add the sand and pumice and stir until thick. (The sand will sink unless you stir diligently!) Pour into molds.

OATMEAL SOAP

Here's a recipe for a classic, old-fashioned skin cleanser that is also soothing to irritated skin.

Ingredients
- 3/4 to 1 cup (102 to 136 g) oatmeal
- Several drops of cinnamon fragrance (optional)

Method

Grind the oats in a blender until the flakes are about one-fifth their original size. Melt together the basic soap and water in a saucepan. Add the oatmeal and stir until the soap is thick enough to prevent the oatmeal from settling to the bottom. Scent very lightly if desired and pour into molds.

GOLDEN MAIZE ABRASIVE SOAP

The cornmeal in these bars is a vigorous abrasive and makes a soap that is suitable for cleaning clogged pores.

Ingredients
• 1-2 to 2/3 cup (66 to 87 g) cornmeal

Method
Melt the basic soap and water together in a saucepan. Add the cornmeal and stir until slightly thickened. Pour into molds.

BRAN SOAP

This recipe makes a gentle abrasive soap for sensitive skin.

Ingredients
- 3/4 to 1 cup (107 to 142 g) oat or wheat bran

Method
Melt the basic soap and water together in a saucepan. Add the bran and stir until slightly thickened. Pour into molds.

WHEAT GERM AND HONEY SOAP

Honey and wheat-germ oil add extra skin-softening power to this mildly abrasive soap.

Ingredients

- 3/4 to 1 cup (46 to 61 g) wheat germ
- 1/4 cup (59 ml) honey
- 2 teaspoons (10 ml) wheat-germ oil

Method

Melt the basic soap and water together in a saucepan. Stir in the wheat germ, honey, and wheat-germ oil, scorching slightly if a golden color is desired. Stir until the soap is cool and thick enough to keep the honey from settling to the bottom. Pour into molds.

Herbal Soaps

What gardener wouldn't enjoy receiving these soaps as gifts? Each bar gains special qualities from the herbs included in it; some herbs are skin softeners, for example, and others are slightly astringent.

SAGE SOAP

This fragrant herb makes a mildly antiseptic soap. For the best results, use rubbed sage, which is very finely powdered.

Ingredients
• 1 to 2 tablespoons (6 to 12 g) rubbed sage

Method
In a saucepan, melt together the basic soap and water. Add the sage, stirring well to distribute. Pour into molds.

CHAMOMILE SOAP

This exceptionally soothing soap gets a special lift from its lemon fragrance, but shouldn't be used by people who are allergic to pollen. By all means use the dried chamomile that comes in tea bags.

Ingredients
- 1 cup (23 g) fresh chopped or dried powdered chamomile flowers
- 1 teaspoon (2 g) powdered ginger
- Pale yellow dye (optional)
- Several drops of lemon fragrance

Method
Melt together the basic soap and water in a saucepan. Stir in the chamomile flowers and ginger. Add the dye, if desired, and the fragrance and pour into molds.

GLYCERIN AND ROSE WATER SOAP

This classic soap is known for its mild skin-softening effects.

Ingredients

- 9 ounces (255 g) purchased or prepared rose water
- 2 tablespoons (30 ml) glycerin
- Rose-colored dye (optional)
- Several drops of rose fragrance (optional)

Method for Making Rose Water

To prepare rose water, first gather fresh rose blossoms; do this during the morning, after the dew as evaporated. Place the petals in a glass, stainless steel, or enamel saucepan and cover them with distilled water. Weigh the floating petals down with a heat-resistant glass dish.

Place the pan over low heat and allow the pot to release steam for at least an hour. You should begin to see drops of rose oil floating on the surface of the water. Do not allow the water to boil.

When the water has taken on a rosy hue, feels thick and soft, and shows evidence of rose oil on its surface, strain the liquid through a tea strainer, using your fingers to press all the liquid from the petals. Store in refrigerator. (Note that rose water may be used as a skin toner; apply to the face with a cotton ball.)

Method for Making Soap

Melt the basic soap and rose water together in a saucepan; note that no water is required. Add the glycerin, stir well, and add the dye and fragrance if desired. (Freshly prepared rose water made from red roses will do a good job of coloring this soap, so you may wish to leave out the extra dye.) Pour into molds.

CALENDULA SOAP

Calendula is one of the most effective herbal skin softeners and has been used for centuries. If this recipe is made with one of the milder basic soaps, it yields a superb facial cleanser for people with delicate skin.

Ingredients
- 1 cup (23 g) prepared fresh or dried calendula flowers
- Several drops of floral fragrance (optional)

Method
Remove the fresh or dried petals from the flower heads. If you're working with purchased heads, you may also need to remove the seeds, which are hard and crescent shaped. Melt together the basic soap and water in a saucepan. Add the calendula petals, stirring well to distribute and soften them. Add fragrance if desired and pour into molds.

ROSEMARY SOAP

Because rosemary is slightly astringent, this soap makes a good body bar for people with oily skin.

Ingredients

- 1 to 2 tablespoons (6 to 12 g) dried ground rosemary or finely chopped fresh rosemary leaves
- Several drops of herbal fragrance (optional)

Method

Melt together the soap and water in a saucepan. Add the rosemary, stirring well to distribute it. Stir in a few drops of herbal fragrance if desired. Pour into molds.

FIELDS OF LAVENDER SOAP

Almost everyone you know is likely to love the fragrance of this traditional soap.

Ingredients

- 3/4 to 1 cup (20 to 27 g) fresh or dried lavender flowers
- Several drops of lavender fragrance
- Lavender or purple dye

Method

Grind the fresh or dried flowers in a blender until fine. Melt together the basic soap and water in a saucepan. When the soap has melted thoroughly, stir in the ground flowers and fragrance. Add just enough dye to color the soap slightly. Pour into molds.

ALOE VERA BARS

Aloe vera is legendary for its soothing effect on the skin.

Ingredients

- 3/4 cup (184 g) purchased aloe vera gel or freshly prepared aloe vera puree
- Light green dye (optional)

Method

To prepare fresh gel, pick and wash six to ten whole stems of aloe. Cut into small pieces and puree the pieces in a blender, making sure that all large pieces are pureed and that a gel results; do not add water. Place the grated basic soap in a saucepan. Measure 3/4 cup of aloe gel (fresh or purchased) and add water until you have a 9-ounce (255 g) total. Stir this mixture into the soap and heat until the soap has melted completely. Add dye if desired and pour the soap into molds.

MARSHMALLOW BARS

Althaea officinalis, *commonly known as marshmallow root, used to be a key ingredient of marshmallows. These early forebears of our contemporary confections were thought of as medicinal but pleasant-tasting candies and were eaten to help ease the symptoms of colds and bronchial conditions. As a skin softener, the root is very effective— and too little known.*

Ingredients
- 1/4 cup (14 g) granular dried marshmallow root or 1/2 cup (28 g) thinly sliced, fresh marshmallow root
- Several drops of patchouli or vanilla fragrance

Method
Place the sliced fresh root or granular dried root in a saucepan, with just enough water to cover. Simmer, covered, for 15 minutes over low heat. Cool the mixture and then liquefy in a blender. Strain and retain the liquid. Place the basic soap, marshmallow liquid, and water in a saucepan, substituting the marshmallow liquid for its weight in water. Stir well and add the fragrance before pouring into molds.

Skin-Softening Soaps

Test these recipes until you find the one that best suits your skin, but be sure to pick more than one favorite! A sampling of these soaps makes a fine gift for anyone with dry or sensitive skin.

VITAMIN E BARS

Vitamin E is a wonderful skin softener. You may make this soap with or without the aloe vera gel.

Ingredients

- 1/4 to 1/2 cup (61 to 122 g) freshly prepared or purchased aloe vera gel
- 1 to 2 ounces (28.4 to 56.7 g) vitamin E oil
- Green dye (optional)

Method

To prepare fresh aloe vera gel, see the instructions for Aloe Vera Bars on page 66. Place the basic soap in a saucepan. Weigh the gel and add water to make a total of 9 ounces (255 g). Stir this mixture into the soap and heat until melted. Then add the vitamin E oil—and dye if desired—and stir well. Pour into molds.

MILK AND HONEY SOAP

The combination of milk and honey is an age-old recipe for softening the skin. The soap itself is fairly soft and retains a pleasant honey aroma.

Ingredients

- 1/4 cup (39 g) instant powdered milk
- 1/4 to 1/2 cup (59 to 118 ml) honey

Method

Melt together the basic soap and 6 ounces (170 g) of water. Add the instant milk, mashing any lumps with the back of your spoon. Add the honey and stir well. (To emphasize the golden color, add the honey and then scorch the mixture slightly by continuing to heat the soap.) Stir until the soap is fairly thick in order to prevent the honey from settling to the bottom. Pour into molds.

BORAX SOAP

Borax is a sodium compound that is often used to soften water and as a whitener in cosmetics. Overdoing it with this additive may cause your soap to curdle, however, so do be careful. You may notice a change in texture in your soap; the borax will make it a bit fluffy.

Ingredients

• 1-1/2 tablespoons (17 g) borax

Method

Melt together the basic soap and water. Add the borax and stir well. Pour into molds.

COCOA BUTTER SOAP

Cocoa butter is recognized universally as a skin emollient. This recipe is very gentle on sensitive skins.

Ingredients
• 1 ounce (28.4 g) cocoa butter

Method
Melt together the basic soap and water. In a small pan, melt the cocoa butter. Add the butter to the soap mixture and stir well. Pour into molds.

BUTTERMILK BARS OR GOAT'S MILK SOAP

Milk and buttermilk have been used as cleansers for centuries. Be sure to use the freshest dairy products possible and take care to dry these soaps quickly and thoroughly. Both goat's milk and buttermilk are good choices for sensitive skins.

Ingredients

- 9 ounces (255 g) buttermilk or goat's milk
- 2 teaspoons (4.5 g) powdered benzoin
- Several drops of peppermint fragrance

Method

Soften the basic soap over low heat. Gradually stir in the buttermilk or goat's milk. When the soap has melted completely, add the benzoin and just enough peppermint fragrance to impart a light fragrance. (Without the added fragrance, this soap may have a slightly sour odor.) Pour into molds.

SUPERFATTED SOAP

Superfatted soaps are rich in skin-softening oils. If you have a history of allergies, however, avoid using lanolin!

Ingredients
- 1 ounce (28.4 g) cocoa butter
- 1 ounce (28.4 g) sweet almond or wheat-germ oil
- 1 ounce (28.4 g) lanolin
- 1 ounce (28.4 g) glycerin

Method
Using only 7 ounces (198 g) of water, melt the basic soap and water together. Melt the cocoa butter in a small pan. Add the almond or wheat-germ oil, the lanolin, and the glycerin to the cocoa butter and mix until all the ingredients have softened. Then add the contents of the saucepan to the soap and stir until slightly thickened. Pour into molds.

Vegetable Soaps

For centuries, vegetables have been used as cosmetics and as skin preparations. Why? Because they work and are inexpensive. The gentle and mild qualities of vegetable soaps make them tempting possibilities for the gift basket, too.

CUCUMBER SOAP

Cucumbers make a good skin cleanser, especially for the face. Select firm cucumbers with dark green skins.

Ingredients

- 1 medium to large cucumber
- 2 teaspoons (4.5 g) powdered benzoin

Method

Remove the ends from the cucumber, slice it lengthwise, and remove the seeds. Liquefy the slices in a blender; do not add water. Weigh the cucumber puree, and add water to make 9 ounces (255 g). Melt the liquid together with the basic soap. Add the benzoin and stir well. Pour into molds.

CARROT SOAP

Carrot soap is a wonderful orange color and contains plenty of vitamin A, which is essential for soft, healthy skin.

Ingredients

- 1 medium to large carrot
- 2 teaspoons (4.5 g) powdered benzoin

Method

Slice the carrot thinly and place in a blender along with just enough water to enable you to liquefy it. Then liquefy and run through a tea strainer, saving the juice and pulp in separate containers. Weigh the juice, adding water to make 9 ounces (255 g). Melt the juice and water together with the basic soap. Stir in 2 tablespoons (30 ml) of the pulp and 2 teaspoons of benzoin. Pour into molds.

LETTUCE SOAP

When added to soap, lettuce makes one of the mildest skin cleansers available.

Ingredients

- 4 to 8 leaves of dark green lettuce
- 2 teaspoons (4.5 g) powdered benzoin
- Pale green dye (optional)

Method

Tear the lettuce leaves into small pieces and place them in a blender. Add just enough water to enable you to liquefy them. Then liquefy, and weigh the lettuce juice, adding water to make 9 ounces (255 g). Melt this mixture together with the basic soap. Add the benzoin, and the dye if desired; stir well. Pour into molds.

Fruit Soaps

Fruit soaps are a great deal of fun to make and share with friends. Although many fruits make interesting and mildly astringent soaps, the ones in these recipes have traditional histories as cosmetics and skin preparations—and are widely available. To prevent spoilage, be sure to dry these soaps as thoroughly and as quickly as possible.

AVOCADO SOAP

Avocados contribute both their green color and skin-softening properties to soaps made with them.

Ingredients

- 1 avocado, ripened
- 1 teaspoon (2 g) powdered benzoin

Method

Remove the pit from the avocado, scrape the pulp from the skin, and mash the pulp until smooth. Weigh the pulp and add water to make 9 ounces (255 g). Melt this mixture together with the basic soap. Add the benzoin and stir well to distribute evenly. Pour into molds.

APRICOT SOAP

Apricots add skin-softening properties and make a rich, creamy soap.

Ingredients

- 9 to 12 dried apricots
- 2 teaspoons (4.5 g) powdered benzoin
- Several drops of patchouli fragrance
- Peach dye (optional)

Method

Cover the apricots with boiling water. Let them stand until they are soft. Then place the apricots and water in a blender and liquefy. Weigh the liquid and add water if necessary to make 9 ounces (255 g). Melt this together with the basic soap. Add the benzoin, the patchouli fragrance, and, if desired, the peach dye, stirring well as you do. Pour into molds.

LEMON NUTMEG GLYCERIN BARS

This soap is wonderful for slightly problematic skins; the glycerin softens the skin as the lemon tightens the pores.

Ingredients

- Juice of one lemon
- 1 ounce (28.5 g) glycerin
- Grated rind of one lemon rind
- 1 to 2 teaspoons (2 to 4 g) ground nutmeg
- Several drops of lemon fragrance

Method

Weigh the lemon juice and add water to make 9 ounces (255 g). Melt the liquid together with the basic soap. Add the glycerin, lemon rind, nutmeg, and fragrance, stirring well as you do. Pour into molds.

TRIPLE LEMON SOAP

This fruity concoction is a good skin cleanser. The lemon peel in it is moderately astringent as well as fragrant.

Ingredients

- Juice of two lemons
- Grated rind of two lemons
- Several drops of lemon fragrance
- 1 teaspoon (2 g) powdered benzoin

Method

Weigh the lemon juice and add water to make 9 ounces (255 g). Melt the liquid together with the basic soap. Add the lemon peel, fragrance, and benzoin, and stir well. Pour into molds.

STRAWBERRY BARS

Strawberries, which are both acidic and astringent, lend remarkably refreshing qualities to this soap.

Ingredients

- 12 to 15 strawberries
- 2 teaspoons (4.5 g) benzoin powder
- Red dye (optional)
- Several drops of strawberry fragrance

Method

Puree the strawberries in a blender; do not add water. Weigh the puree and add water to make 9 ounces (255 g). Melt the liquid together with the basic soap. Add the benzoin, dye, if desired, and fragrance, stirring well as you do. Pour into molds.

KIWI BARS

Kiwis are filled with skin-nurturing vitamins and minerals. Bars of this soap will be a rich green color.

Ingredients

- 1 kiwi
- 2 teaspoons (4.5 g) powdered benzoin
- Several drops of ylang ylang fragrance
- Green dye (optional)

Method

Peel the kiwi. Slice, place in a blender, and puree; do not add water. Weigh the pureed kiwi and add water to make 9 ounces (255 g). Melt the liquid together with the basic soap. Add the benzoin, fragrance, and, if desired, green dye, stirring well as you do. Pour into molds.

Spice Soaps

To help fill your soap-maker's closet, why not turn to the spice rack? Many common culinary spices serve as wonderful additions to soaps, and some even add lather as well as fragrance and color.

GINGER BARS

Try this refreshing and distinctively fragrant soap on a cold winter's night; the ginger in it will warm your skin. This soap has a mild, spicy aroma even without added fragrances.

Ingredients
- 2 teaspoons (4 g) powdered ginger
- Yellow dye (optional)
- Several drops of sassafras fragrance (optional)

Method

Melt together the basic soap and water. Add the ginger, the yellow dye, if desired, and the fragrance; stir well. Pour into molds.

CLOVE SOAP

Cloves add an invigorating touch to soap, but measure carefully; too many cloves can actually irritate your skin!

Ingredients

- 1/2 to 1 teaspoon (1 to 2 g) ground cloves
- Several drops of clove oil (optional)

Method

Melt together the basic soap and water. Add the ground cloves; for a stronger fragrance, also add the clove oil. Stir well and pour into molds.

CINNAMON SOAP

Cinnamon soap is a real pick-me-up. The dark brown bars lather very generously indeed and have a spicy aroma.

Ingredients

- 2 teaspoons (4 g) ground cinnamon
- Several drops of cinnamon fragrance

Method

Melt together the basic soap and water. Add the cinnamon and the fragrance oil, and stir well. Pour into molds.

ORANGE-BLOSSOM POMANDER BARS

With its traditional holiday scent, this soap makes a great Christmas gift.

Ingredients
- 1-1/2 teaspoons (3 g) ground cinnamon
- 1 teaspoon (2 g) ground ginger
- Several drops of neroli and cinnamon fragrance
- 2 tablespoons (14 g) ground orange or lemon peel, fresh or dry

Method
Melt together the basic soap and water. Add the cinnamon, orange or lemon peel, and ginger, and stir well. Add the fragrances, stir again, and pour into molds.

Other Additive Soaps

These recipes just don't fit into convenient categories, but every one of them yields an interesting soap with a purpose.

FRENCH CLAY BARS

French clay is a cosmetic clay which removes oils and impurities from oily skin. The powdered clay, available at health-food stores, comes in green, red, or beige.

Ingredients
• 1 to 2 tablespoons (11 to 23 g) French clay

Method
Melt together the basic soap and water. Stir in the clay very well. Pour into molds.

ROSIN BARS

Rosin is commonly used in soaps as a stiffener (it hardens the bars) and as an aid to the cleansing process. This recipe is old-fashioned—and reliable!

Ingredients
• 1 tablespoon (9 g) powdered rosin

Method
Melt together the basic soap and water. Sprinkle the rosin over the top and stir it in well to distribute it evenly. Pour into molds.

ENGLISH FLOWER-GARDEN BARS

Although the fresh flower petals in this soap will change colors once they've been incorporated, the bars are nevertheless very pretty. During the summer, fresh carnations, roses, and daisies will work well; try mum or aster petals during the fall. You may substitute dried petals if you wish.

Ingredients
• 1 cup (27 g) fresh or dried flower petals

Method
Melt together the basic soap and water. Stir in the petals until the soap is speckled throughout. Pour into molds.

SCANDINAVIAN BIRCH-LEAF SOAP

Since ancient times, Scandinavians, Russians, and Germans have recognized the curative powers of oil of birch. The oil is reputed to cure eczema and other skin afflictions, and you'll also find that it warms the skin.

Ingredients
• 1 teaspoon (5 ml) birch-leaf oil

Method
Melt together the basic soap and water. Add the oil of birch and stir well. Pour into molds.

MEDICATED SOAP

Sulfur, which is for external use only, has been used for hundreds of years as a mild antiseptic and as a healing medicament for the skin. This soap will have a characteristic sulfur odor; to mask that odor, use a fragrance.

Ingredients
- 1-1/2 tablespoons (10 g) flowers of sulfur
- Several drops of any fragrance

Method
Melt together the basic soap and water. Sprinkle in the sulfur, stirring it well to distribute it evenly. Pour into molds.

SKIN BALM BARS

This soap combines the softening effects of calendula with the legendary healing qualities of tea-tree oil. In a mild basic soap, these additives should prove soothing to skin rashes.

Ingredients
- 1 tablespoon (15 ml) tea-tree oil
- 3 ounces (85 g) calendula flowers
- 1 teaspoon (2 g) powdered benzoin

Method
Melt together the basic soap and water. Blend in the tea-tree oil and then add the calendula flowers and benzoin, stirring well as you do. Pour into molds.

ODOR-EATING SOAP

Coffee grounds are reputed to remove kitchen odors from your hands. My surveys show that some people swear by it, while others are unimpressed. The next time you peel onions or garlic, try this soap for yourself!

Ingredients
- 3 tablespoons (20 g) freshly ground coffee
- 1 teaspoon (2 g) powdered benzoin

Method
Melt together the basic soap and water. Add the coffee and benzoin. Stir until the soap is cool so the grounds will not sink to the bottom of the molds. Pour into molds.

WOODSMAN'S SOAP

The four oils in this recipe are all reputed to have insect-repellent qualities. If one doesn't work, the others should! To reap the soap's cumulative effects, use it repeatedly over a period of time.

Ingredients
- 1 teaspoon (5 ml) citronella oil
- 1 teaspoon (5 ml) lavender oil
- 1 teaspoon (5 ml) lemon oil
- 2 teaspoons (10 ml) cedar leaf oil

Method
Melt together the basic soap and water. Add the oils and stir well to distribute them evenly. Pour into molds.

WITCH HAZEL SOAP

Because it is a mild astringent, witch hazel in a skin-drying basic soap such as Cocoa Creme (see page 42) will yield a milled soap that is especially good for oily skin. Even people with sensitive skin can use this soap, but should do so only occasionally.

Ingredients
• 9 ounces (255 g) witch hazel

Method
Melt the basic soap and the witch hazel together in a saucepan, stirring thoroughly to distribute the witch hazel evenly. (Note that no water is necessary in this recipe.) Pour into molds.

THREE KINGS ANTIBACTERIAL SOAP

A pleasantly scented hand soap for kitchen or bath, this soap combines the scent of the Middle East with the antibacterial qualities of myrrh.

Ingredients
- 2 teaspoons (4 g) frankincense powder
- Several drops of sandalwood fragrance
- 1 tablespoon (13 g) powdered myrrh

Method
Melt together the basic soap and water. Add the frankincense powder and stir well. Add the fragrance and myrrh, stirring to distribute evenly. Pour into molds.

FISHERMAN'S SOAP

Many fishermen believe that fish are attracted to anise oil, and some research indicates that this may be true. Although we make no promises here regarding your catch of the day, you or your favorite angler may want to sample this soap anyway. Try washing your fishing gear in it, too!

Ingredients
- 1 tablespoon (15 ml) anise oil
- Blue dye (optional)

Method
Melt together the basic soap and water. Add the anise oil, stirring it in well. Add the dye if desired and pour into molds.

GARDEN-OF-THE-SEA SOAP

When made with a mild basic soap, this personal favorite of mine is exceptionally gentle, and its slippery texture reminds me of ocean water. Due to its pale green color, the soap is fun to mold into the shapes of water-loving creature such as frogs.

Ingredients
- 1 to 2 tablespoons (14 to 27 g) powdered kelp
- Several drops of any fragrance

Method
Melt together the basic soap and water. Sprinkle the kelp over the top and stir it in well for even distribution. Add the fragrance and stir in thoroughly. Pour into molds.

BALSAMIC SOAP

Balsam of Peru is a sticky, viscous liquid with a warm, vanilla-like scent. A mild antiseptic, it has been used for centuries in cosmetics and for skin eruptions. When made with a mild basic soap, this recipe should yield soothing bars for anyone with skin problems.

Ingredients
• 3 tablespoons (45 ml) balsam of Peru

Method
Melt together the basic soap and water. Add the balsam of Peru and stir it in well to distribute it evenly. Pour into molds.

Chapter Eight:
Specialty Soaps

By now you've probably realized that one of the more enjoyable aspects of making soap is being able to select recipes to suit your particular needs. This chapter extends that opportunity by providing instructions for a number of specialty soaps, including shampoos (for people and their animal friends), liquid soaps and gels, and translucent soaps.

SHAMPOOS FOR YOU
(AND THE FAMILY DOG)

A good shampoo produces suds, and the ingredient which best creates suds is coconut oil. The three shampoos described in this section—one for dry to normal hair, one for oily hair, and one for the canines of your acquaintance—all include coconut oil, but their other ingredients vary.

To make either of the two shampoos for humans, follow the "Master Instructions for Shampoo" (see opposite page) using the ingredients listed for the shampoo you've selected. These instructions will walk you through the steps necessary to make either a hard shampoo bar or a "squeezable" shampoo.

No matter what shampoo you use, your hair should always be rinsed with an acidic hair rinse before you leave the shower. You'll find a wonderful recipe for an herbal rinse on page 104.

To make the shampoo for dogs, simply choose one of the two shampoo recipes and follow the "Master Instructions for Shampoo," but substitute the additives listed under "Dog Shampoo."

Dog Shampoo

Use this shampoo, which will repel fleas and other insects, only on the animals for which it's named—not on cats! Study your dog's coat and choose the herbal shampoo recipe that best suits the condition of that coat. Then follow the "Master Instructions for Shampoo," but substitute the oils listed here for the rosemary, chamomile, and cinnamon-leaf oils listed in the basic recipes. Be careful not to exceed the recommended amounts of oils, or you may make this shampoo too strong.

Ingredients

- 1 quart (946 ml) of either liquid shampoo
- 2 drops pennyroyal or peppermint oil
- 2 drops lemon oil
- 2 drops lavender oil
- 2 drops cedarwood oil

Herbal Essence Shampoo for Dry to Normal Hair

This shampoo is certainly mild enough for everyday use, but be sure to work it into your hair thoroughly and rinse your hair well. If your hair defies description—if it's oily here and dry there—you can avoid stripping the natural oils from it by using this shampoo on one hair-washing day and the shampoo for oily hair on the next.

Ingredients

- 10 ounces (283 g) coconut oil
- 6 ounces (170 g) tallow
- 4 ounces (113 g) castor oil
- 34 ounces (964 g) olive oil
- 7 ounces (198 g) lye
- 20-1/2 ounces (581 g) water
- 3 to 6 drops of rosemary oil (for dark hair) or chamomile oil (for light hair)
- Several drops of pine fragrance

Herbal Essence Shampoo for Oily Hair

Here's a shampoo that leaves oily hair clean and soft. I have rather dry hair with split ends, but I still use this recipe once in awhile to rid my scalp of oily build-up.

Ingredients

- 16 ounces (454 g) coconut oil
- 4 ounces (113 g) castor oil
- 34 ounces (964 g) olive oil
- 7 ounces (198 g) lye
- 20-1/2 ounces (581 g) water
- 3 to 6 drops of cinnamon-leaf oil
- Several drops of pine fragrance

Soap played an important role in the development of advertising. Until the late 1800s, most advertisements touted the benefits of patent medicines or announced the arrival of the circus. By the 1880s, however, soap manufacturers were distributing cards to advertise their products; these included the name of the soap, a picture, and a pithy phrase that would help customers to remember the particular product. These slogan-bearing cards and special offers made by soap manufacturers were precursors to modern advertising techniques.

MASTER INSTRUCTIONS FOR SHAMPOO

TIP ~ *When making shampoo—either hard bars or liquid shampoo—it's best to grate and remelt the basic soap as soon as possible.*

What You Need

- Equipment for making basic soap (see page 33) and hand-milled soap (see page 49)
- 4-quart (3.8 l) stainless steel, enamel, or glass saucepan
- Ingredients for selected shampoo recipe
- 1/2 teaspoon (1 g) powdered pectin, for liquid shampoo
- Empty plastic shampoo bottle
- 1 gallon (3.8 l) vinegar or juice bottle

Method

1. Follow Steps 1 through 13 of the "Master Instructions for Basic Soaps" on pages 33-35, using the fats and/or oils and lye listed in your selected shampoo recipe, but bring the temperatures of both the lye solution and of the fats and/or oils to 95°F (35°C). Then continue with Steps 14 and 15. Both recipes provided in this section are high in liquid oils, so you'll need to stir quite a bit.

2. When the shampoo has thickened and shows trailings, pour it into a primary mold, and wrap it in insulating materials as if you were making a batch of basic soap. Allow the shampoo to set up until it is hard enough to be grated.

3. After the shampoo has set up, remove it from the primary mold. To make hardened, milled shampoo bars, continue to Step 4. To make a liquid shampoo, skip Step 4 and continue to Steps 5 and 6.

4. To make shampoo bars, mill the block of basic soap just as you would when making any hand-milled soap recipe (see the "Master Instructions for Hand-Milled Soaps" on pages 48-51). When the remelted soap shows trailings, add 3 to 6 drops of the appropriate oil (chamomile, rosemary, or cinnamon-leaf) and several drops of pine fragrance just before pouring the soap into molds. Note that you may use individual molds to make fancy shampoo bars or you may pour your milled soap into a primary mold, allow it to set up, and slice it into hefty rectangular or square bars.

5. To make a smooth, squeezable shampoo, mix together the following ingredients in a saucepan: 5 ounces (142 g) of the grated block of basic soap; 30 ounces (851 g) of water; and 1/2 teaspoon (1 g) of powdered pectin. (Omitting the pectin will cause the shampoo to separate in the bottle, leaving big chunks of floating soap.) Heat the mixture until it is smooth and liquid. Then add 3 to 6 drops of chamomile, rosemary, or cinnamon leaf oil, and several drops of pine fragrance. Too much of any of these oils can irritate the skin, so do measure carefully, and shake the shampoo bottle thoroughly before each use.

6. Fill your empty plastic shampoo bottle with the soft shampoo and store the remaining shampoo in the large, tightly sealed vinegar or juice bottle. Refill the smaller plastic bottle from the large bottle as necessary.

HERB AND VINEGAR HAIR RINSE

Hair rinses serve to return your hair to its natural pH (acidity level) after shampooing. A good hair rinse will also bring out the highlights in your hair and will enhance its natural color.

To make a rinse that is tailored to your type of hair, study the list below and select any herb or combination of herbs that fit your hair type and purpose.

Sage
color enhancement for dark hair

Chamomile
color enhancement for light hair

Thyme
dandruff control for all types

Rosemary
brightener for dull hair

Nettles
conditioner for all types

If your hair is damaged or you spend a great deal of time outdoors, gathering fresh stinging nettles (*Urtica dioica*) for use as a conditioner is well worth the trouble. The plant's stems and leaves are covered with spines that deliver a painful sting on contact, so wear gloves and use pruners to cut the stalks at the base. Place the nettles where they can dry undisturbed. The dry plants can be handled with bare hands.

What You Need

- 4-quart (3.8 l) stainless steel, enamel, or glass saucepan
- Tea strainer or sieve
- Mixing bowl
- Clean, empty shampoo bottle
- Small plastic dispenser bottle

Ingredients

- A few handfuls of any herb or combination of herbs selected from the list above.
- 3 tablespoons (45 ml) cider vinegar

Method

1. Collect and rinse your fresh herbs and allow them to drip dry.

2. Place several handfuls of leaves and stems into the saucepan. Fill the pan with water and place the pan over medium-high heat.

3. Bring the contents to a boil, remove the saucepan from the heat, and allow the contents to cool completely.

4. Strain the contents through a tea strainer or sieve and into a mixing bowl, reserving the liquid only.

5. Place the cider vinegar into the shampoo bottle and fill the bottle with the herbal liquid.

6. This hair rinse must be kept cool to prevent it from fermenting. For use in the shower, fill your small plastic dispenser bottle from the larger bottle; store the large bottle in the refrigerator. To use the hair rinse, first shampoo and rinse your hair. Then saturate your hair completely with the herbal rinse and towel or air-dry it without removing the rinse. The mild vinegar odor will fade away quickly.

LIQUID SOAPS AND SOAP GELS

Commercially produced liquid soaps have become quite popular in recent years, although most are actually detergents rather than soaps. The instructions provided here may be modified to yield either true liquid soap, which can be pumped smoothly out of a bottle, or a gel soap firm enough to be placed in containers and dipped out by hand.

TIPS

■ The proportions of soap and water in this recipe are approximate. You may need to experiment a little with them in order to achieve the correct consistency for your gel or liquid soap.

■ Don't make liquid soaps or gels too far in advance, or they'll dry out. To keep the contents of liquid soaps smooth enough to flow freely from the soap bottle, shake the bottle once every few days. Keep soap gels in containers with lids.

■ When making liquid soaps, avoid using heavy additives such as oatmeal, which will simply sink to the bottom of the bottle. Gel soaps will accept heavier additives more readily.

■ For people whose hands get really dirty, sand and pumice—both of which are abrasive—serve as popular additives in gel soaps.

What You Need
- Equipment for making basic soap (see page 33) and hand-milled soap (see page 49)
- 2-quart (1.9 l) stainless steel, enamel, or glass saucepan.
- Small dish

Liquid Soap Ingredients
- 2 ounces (56.7 g) grated basic soap of your choice
- 8 ounces (227 g) water
- Additives, if desired, as listed in any hand-milled soap recipe

Soap Gel Ingredients
- 2 ounces (56. 7 g) grated basic soap of your choice
- 5 ounces (142 g) water
- Additives, if desired, as listed in any hand-milled soap recipe

Method

1. Select a basic soap recipe and a hand-milled soap recipe (see Chapters Five and Seven). Make a batch of the basic soap, then grate the soap and permit it to dry for only a few days. Measure 12 ounces (340 g) of grated soap and mix in any additives, fragrances, and/or colors, making sure to add them in the proportions given in your selected hand-milled soap recipe.

2. Place the grated soap and water in a saucepan. Note that soap gels require less water than do liquid soaps.

3. Heat the mixture gently, trying not to stir too vigorously. To help the soap melt completely, use a whisk to break up any small pieces.

4. When the soap has melted, check its consistency by placing a spoonful in a small dish and cooling the dish in a cold-water bath. If the soap seems too thin or too thick at room temperature, add a little more water or grated soap, and reheat if necessary.

5. When its consistency is correct, pour the soap into the container of your choice.

TRANSLUCENT SOAPS

Every would-be soap maker dreams of making translucent soaps—more commonly known as glycerin soaps. (I've always thought this a misnomer; all the homemade soaps described in this books are glycerin soaps!) These bars are so intriguing that once you've made them, you may have trouble bringing yourself to use them or give them away.

The addition of 80-proof liquor is absolutely necessary in this recipe; either 80-proof vodka or 80-proof whiskey will work. The latter will make amber-colored bars, while vodka will make a soap that is easier to color to your specifications. After you've made this soap a few times, you'll find yourself watching the liquor-store ads for specials! (Never use isopropyl or other forms of alcohol as they are highly flammable at relatively low temperatures and can cause the melting soap ingredients to catch fire.)

To assure the best possible results, mold translucent soaps in attractive, guest-sized bars or large, bold rectangular and oval bars. You may also want to scent these soaps, as without added fragrance, they have a distinctive smell of their own, one which some people think is reminiscent of alcohol! To tell the truth, it reminds me of limes.

Do follow the directions carefully, as deviation from them may result in a soap that is cloudy rather than translucent. Remember to keep your expectations realistic, too; even when it's made properly, this soap is translucent, not clear.

TIP—*Don't forget to measure your vodka or whiskey by weight, not by volume!*

What You Need

- Equipment for making basic soap (see page 33)
- 4-quart (3.8 l) stainless steel, enamel, or glass saucepan
- Shot glass

Ingredients

- 16 ounces (454 g) coconut oil
- 6 ounces (170 g) tallow
- 2 four-ounce (113 g) bottles of castor oil
- 4 ounces (113 g) lye
- 10 ounces (283 g) water
- 8 ounces (227 g) granulated sugar
- 10 ounces (283 g) 80-proof vodka or whiskey
- Dye (optional)
- Several drops of any fragrance (optional)

Method

1. Using the oils, fats, lye, and water listed under "Ingredients" above, follow Steps 1 through 17 of the "Master Instructions for Basic Soaps" on pages 33-36.

2. Allow the soap to set up for a day or two, then remove it from the primary mold. Don't worry if the soap is still soft; just pry it out of the mold.

3. Slice, mash, or grate the soap into very small pieces.

4. Place the soap in the saucepan. Using an over-sized pan for this step will only tempt you to overstir the soap!

5. Place the saucepan over very low heat. Heat the soap until it softens or melts, but don't allow it to come to a boil. Aim for a very gentle simmer instead; the soap should bubble just a bit. The more vigorous the bubbling action, the poorer the results.

6. As the soap begins to melt, add the granulated sugar and the 80-proof whiskey or vodka. Mix these in as gently as possible. This soap contains so much coconut oil that overstirring it will produce a lot of suds, which will interfere with the clearing process.

7. Simmer the soap gently for about ten minutes. You'll notice a scum forming on top. Push this aside; you should see clear soap in the bottom of the pan. If the soap is still cloudy, remove and discard this scum. It's entirely possible to remove the soap from the heat too soon, before the alcohol has had a chance to boil off.

8. To test the soap, ladle a bit of it (without any scum) into a shot glass. Place the glass in the freezer and allow it to cool completely. (Remove the remaining soap from the heat while you wait for your test soap to cool.) If the cool test soap isn't translucent, return the pot of soap to the heat.

9. When you're sure that your soap has cleared, remove it from the heat. Using your stirring spoon, skim off the layer of scum, placing it in a bowl to harden; you can use it later for making Soap Balls (see pages 108-109).

10. If you'd like to add the dye and scent oil to your cleared soap, do so now, stirring them in thoroughly but gently. Pour the soap into individual molds, keeping in mind that the deeper the molds are, the more cloudy the completed soaps will appear. Use thin molds or pour only a thin layer of soap into each one.

SOAP BALLS

Soap balls are found far and wide, but I'd venture to guess that they originated in New England; I tend to think of them as testaments to the stubborn temperament of the Yankee mentality. Attractive and useful, they appeal to the soap maker who can't bear to see that last sliver of soap slip down the drain. Cost-conscious soap makers will rescue these small remnants and give them new life. If you can identify with this urge, you're a true Yankee at heart!

There are several ways to make soap balls, but no matter which method you use, you'll end up with a wonderful collection of attractive soaps.

Old-Fashioned New England Style Soap Balls

Use the instructions that follow to make charming soap balls from your collection of basic or hand-milled soap scraps. I store my scraps in the linen closet, keeping separate those that are natural in color and those that are dyed. Don't mix these together; you won't like the color that results!

What You Need
- Mixing bowl
- Sharp knife
- Stirring spoon

Ingredients
- Shavings, scrapings, or other small soap pieces
- Warm water

Method

1. Place the scraps of soap in a bowl. Break up any large pieces or shave them down with a knife.

2. Sprinkle warm water over the scraps and stir until all the pieces are moistened. Allow ten minutes or so for the soap to soften.

3. Grab a fistful of the moistened scraps and squeeze them together to form a ball. Do be careful to squeeze out any air pockets, or the ball may fall apart once it has dried. Repeat to make as many balls as possible.

4. Place the soap balls in a warm dry area and allow them to dry for two weeks or more. Once every few days, squeeze each soap ball in order to maintain its round shape as it dries.

New-Fangled Soap Balls

If you don't want to wait for months while your soap-scrap collection grows, use one of the following methods to achieve the same results.

Technique #1

When it comes time to pour a batch of hand-milled soap into molds, you'll often find that there's not quite enough soap to fill the very last mold. Use that remaining portion (or an entire soap recipe if you like) to make New-Fangled Soap Balls by shaping the slightly cooled leftover soap into balls. To decorate the balls, roll them in a handful or two of grated soap before setting them aside to dry.

Technique #2

These soap balls are truly old-fashioned in appearance. Just follow your hand-milled soap recipe, but rather than using individual molds, pour the soap into a large mold instead. Freeze the soap until it is solid enough to be removed from the mold, then cut the soap into blocks. Grate each block or shave it into small pieces with a knife and allow the pieces to dry for up to one week in a shallow container. These bits of soap can still be quite moist.

To make the balls, follow the instructions for making Old-Fashioned New England Style Soap Balls.

MODERN soap makers can depend on the consistent strength of the lye they purchase. A century ago, however, the strength of home-made lye was tested by placing an egg in the solution. If the egg floated, the lye was considered to be too strong; if the egg sank, the lye was thought to be too weak. When the lye strength was just right, the egg would float slowly to the bottom—or so folks believed!

SOAP ON A ROPE

Here's an item that you'll find advertised in fancy catalogues.

TIP — *You'll need 2 feet (61 cm) of braided cording for each molded bar of soap. The cording is available at fabric stores*

What You Need
• Equipment for making hand-milled soap (see page 49)
• Scissors
• Braided cording

Ingredients
• A batch of basic soap
• Ingredients for selected hand-milled soap recipe

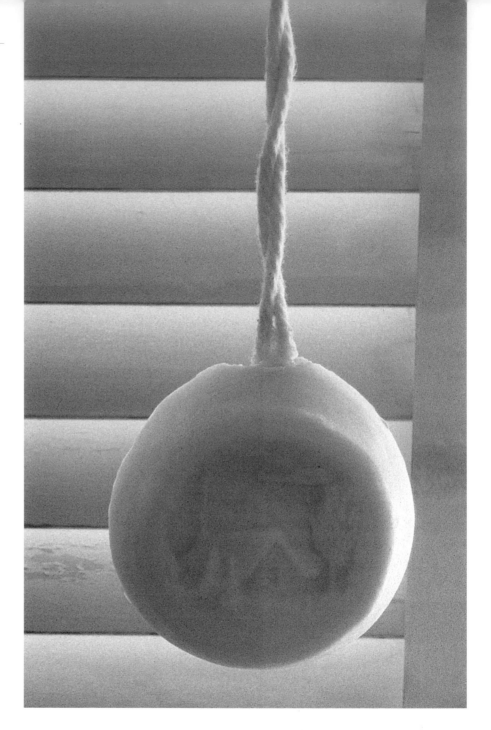

Method

1. Select a hand-milled soap recipe and large, deep molds for the individual bars.

2. Follow Steps 1 through 8 of the "Master Instructions for Hand-Milled Soaps" (see pages 49-50).

3. Pour the soap into the molds until each mold is half filled.

4. Fold each piece of cording double. Cross the two loose ends on top of the layer of soft soap, making sure that these ends, which will be covered by a second layer of soap, are placed at least half-way across the first layer. (Ends that aren't set deeply enough may work loose as the soap is used.) Rest the looped end of each cord on your work surface. Try to keep the cords as clean as possible.

5. Fill the remainder of each mold with soap. Freeze the molds until the soap is solid, then remove the bars from the molds and allow them to dry as usual.

FLOATING SOAP

If your household includes small children, soaps that float (made by beating air into them) are a plus! The following instructions may be used with any basic or milled soap. As you beat the soap, it will cool quickly, so prepare your molds in advance. Have a spatula on hand, too; if the soap gets too thick, you may have to use this utensil to pack it into the molds.

What You Need
• Equipment for making hand-milled soap (see page 49)
• Hand-held mixer
• 2-to 3-quart (1.9 to 2.8 l) stainless steel, enamel, or glass saucepan
• Spatula

Ingredients
• A batch of any basic or hand-milled soap

Method
1. Follow Steps 1 through 3 of the "Master Instructions for Hand-Milled Soaps" (see page 49).

2. Place the grated soap and water in a saucepan large enough to accommodate the beaters of a hand-held mixer. Melt the soap and water together.

3. When the soap and water have melted, beat at high speed for at least two minutes or until the soap begins to thicken and looks frothy and light.

4. Pour or spoon the beaten soap into your molds; don't forget to clean off the beaters before the soap on them hardens! If your soap has thickened so quickly that you have difficulty getting it into the molds, remelt it with a little more water and beat once again.

FLOATING SOAP

Accidents—even in soapmaking—can sometimes be blessings in disguise. Ivory, the famous floating soap, was the result of simple carelessness. A soapmaker left for his break one day, forgetting to turn off the machine that was whipping his batch of soap. The result? Bars of soap so filled with air that they were unsinkable!

MARBLED SOAP

These visually beautiful soaps are made by using a simple marbling technique. You may either use Plain White Soap (see page 39), adding color to a portion of it, or combine two different soaps for special effects.

What You Need

- Equipment for making hand-milled soap (see page 49)
- Small bowl
- Knife or small spatula

Ingredients

- 12 ounces (340 g) Plain White Soap
- 9 ounces (255 g) water
- Dye of your choice

Method

1. Follow Steps 1 through 7 of the "Master Instructions for Hand-Milled Soaps (see pages 49-50). When the soap has melted and is smooth, remove 25 percent from the saucepan and place it in a small bowl.

2. Using the dye of your choice or a colorful additive such as cinnamon, color the soap in the small bowl, stirring the dye in well.

3. Pour the remaining 75 percent of the soap into individual molds or into one large mold. Then pour a small amount of the colored soap into each mold, allowing it to flow in an S-shaped pattern. Continue in this fashion until all of colored soap is used.

4. Using a knife or small spatula, fold the dyed soap throughout the soap in the molds until you've achieved a marbled effect. Make sure that the dyed soap is folded in as deeply as possible.

5. Allow the soap to cool, place the molds in the freezer until the bars have hardened, then remove the bars from the molds as usual.

CONFETTI SOAP

Making this soap is a colorful method for using scraps of hand-milled soaps. You'll find that Confetti Soaps look best when soaps colored with natural dyes are kept separate from synthetically dyed soaps.

What You Need

- Equipment for making hand-milled soap (see page 49)
- Sharp knife

Ingredients

- Two handfuls of hand-milled soap scraps
- 12 ounces (340 g) of any basic soap
- 9 ounces (255 g) water

Method

1. Shave the hand-milled soap scraps into small pieces, each about the size of a chocolate chip.

2. Follow Steps 1 through 7 of the "Master Instructions for Hand-Milled Soaps" (see pages 49-50) to melt together the grated basic soap and water. When the soap has melted, add the scraps and stir them in thoroughly. Pour into molds, freeze the molds, and remove the soaps as usual.

Chapter Nine:

Troubleshooting and Adjustments

You may never have occasion to use this chapter, but if you do, don't feel bad! Even experienced soap makers can run into trouble once in awhile, usually because they've tried to "ad-lib" a recipe or because they've been careless. Old hands, completely familiar with what they're doing, are sometimes even more lax than beginners!

Fortunately, most soap-making errors can be corrected; completely ruining a batch of soap takes real effort. On rare occasions, there's no way to be certain what went wrong. What I've learned—and I'm sure you will too—is how to accept one's mistakes and how to rely on one's experience and instincts.

Following are descriptions of the problems you're most likely to encounter as you make soap, as well as solutions for each one.

COMPLETE SEPARATIONS

PROBLEM: The lye and fat separate in the primary mold; the fats float to the top, and the lye sinks to the bottom.

CAUSE: Inaccurate measurements or cooling too rapidly.

SOLUTION: Reheat the entire mixture to 110°F (43°C) by placing the primary mold in a sink filled with a combination of boiling water and hot tap water. Do not let the temperature of the mixture rise above 120°F (49°C). If the soap is too hard to remelt in this fashion, place it back in your soap pot and heat it up on the stove. In either case, stir the mixture as it melts. When it has melted completely, remove it from the heat and stir it until it begins to show trailings. When it does, pour the soap into the primary mold and rewrap the mold in its insulating blanket.

When you unwrap the soap, if it has only partly blended or has separated again, throw the stuff out! Also discard it if the solid soap that has formed is slimy feeling or will not dry thoroughly. You've probably made mistakes when measuring your ingredients.

If the unwrapped soap looks normal, it was most likely cooled too quickly the first time around.

LAYERING

PROBLEM: As the soap cools in the mold, a layer of oil rises to the top.

CAUSE: Too much oil in a recipe, incorrect proportions, or substitutions of ingredients. Olive Oil Castile Soap is prone to this problem; special instructions for curing it are on page 45.

SOLUTION: Pour off the excess oil and save it for another recipe. Reheat the soap, remove it from the heat, and stir until trailings are visible. Pour the soap into the primary mold and rewrap the mold. When the soap has set up, remove it from the mold and allow it to dry as usual. Check the soap in two to three weeks. If it lathers well and isn't caustic, it is safe to use. If it's still caustic after three weeks, throw the batch of soap away.

CURDLING

PROBLEM: Soap can curdle both when you are making basic soaps and during the remelting stage of making hand-milled soaps. Curdled soap looks like cottage cheese; you'll see solid chunks of soap or fat, which are surrounded by liquid.

CAUSE: Cooling a basic soap too quickly, inaccurately measuring basic soap ingredients, or adding an excess of dyes or additives that contain sodium or sodium compounds to hand-milled soaps.

SOLUTION: Curdling in basic soaps which has been caused by inaccurate measurements is difficult to cure; if you'd like to try anyway, follow the instructions for complete separations. If the cause of the problem in a hand-milled soap is an excessive amount of sodium, you may be able to reclaim your batch of soap by diluting it. Weigh out another batch of basic soap and water, add it to the curdled hand-milled soap, and reheat the combined batches. If the curdling is still severe, discard the soap.

SLIMY SOAP

PROBLEM: You'll recognize slimy soap when you touch it!

CAUSE: Inaccurate measurements or an inaccurate scale.

SOLUTION: None.

LYE BUBBLES

PROBLEM: Lye bubbles aren't usually visible on the outside of the block of basic soap. You'll see them, however, when you cut up the soap block for drying. If you see any pockets of clear liquid, and if you aren't wearing your gloves, put the gloves on right away! The liquid is caustic lye.

CAUSE: An overabundance of lye in the recipe; the lye hasn't been able to find enough oils or fats with which to combine.

SOLUTION: If the bubbles are large, throw the batch away. If the bubbles are very small, proceed as usual, wearing gloves to cut the soap and making sure that you cut it over a sink where the lye can run off without doing any damage. Lightly rinse off the remaining lye or allow it to evaporate as the soap dries.

FREE FAT

PROBLEM: Free fat—fat that hasn't combined with lye—won't be visible to the eye, but your nose will recognize it right away as it tends to go rancid! Soap with free fat won't dry properly either.

CAUSE: Too much fat or too little lye in the recipe.

SOLUTION: Throw offensive smelling soap away.

VARIABILITY FROM BATCH TO BATCH

Soap makers often lament the variations they experience from batch to batch of the same soap recipe. These differences are usually slight, but are visually obvious and sometimes disheartening. Even in my classes, where students work side by side and use the same ingredients, these differences sometimes show up.

Unfortunately, soap making is a sophisticated process and is not entirely under our control. The largest single variable you'll face is the quality of your tallow. The suet you bought and rendered into tallow last week may have come from an animal fed corn and hay. This week, you might have used suet from animals who were pastured or who were fed additional grains. All these factors—and many more—will cause your batches of soap to vary.

On the bright side, chances are that you've chosen to make your own soap because you're tired of the perfectly white, overscented bars available at stores. True soap makers—and you'll soon be one of them—learn to savor variations and to enjoy the sometimes unpredictable results!

REMOVING BLEMISHES

When you're churning out a large number of soaps at one time, small imperfections may escape your notice. If you plan to use these soaps at home, a bump here and there may not matter to you, but you'll probably want your gift soaps to be as close to perfect as possible.

Slight irregularities and warped edges are easily remedied by shaving them away with a vegetable peeler, file, or rasp. If you enjoy working with soaps, by all means try your hand at some simple carving, too. Any small knife is suitable for this purpose.

Sometimes, less obvious blemishes can be smoothed away by dipping a finger into warm water and rubbing the surface of the soap. Occasionally, your soaps may take on the color of a surface they've touched when they were wet. These color spots can usually be washed away under the faucet.

Chapter Ten:

Decorating, Storing, Wrapping, and Displaying

Whether your handmade soaps are destined to be used by your own family, by friends, or by customers, you'll want to be sure that every bar you've made looks its best. In this chapter, you'll find helpful hints on storing, wrapping, and displaying the results of your soapmaking efforts.

APPLYING SOAP DECALS

Making and applying decals to gift soaps is an easy way to enhance their appearance and a great way to keep children busy on a rainy afternoon. Decals are colorful embellishments that will make your soaps real eye-poppers.

The first step is to select a decal. Colorful images cut from magazines, gift wraps, and special-occasion cards work well, as do leaves and flowers that have been pressed and dried. Do avoid cutting decals from paper that is thick and bulky, and make sure that your decals are the correct size for the bars to which they'll be attached. When you're browsing for printed decals, select only those that have clearly defined edges; trying to trim away complex backgrounds can be cumbersome.

For gift soaps, choose decals to match the interests of the people who will be the lucky recipients. A nature-loving friend, for example, is bound to appreciate a gift basket filled with soaps that bear decals based on nature-related themes such as birds, flowers, or animals.

What You Need

- Sharp scissors
- Decal materials
- Bars of soap
- 1-pound (454 g) block of paraffin
- Empty tuna can
- Frying pan
- Small recycled paintbrush
- Baby oil or mineral oil
- Soft cloth or paper towels

Method

1. Using very sharp scissors, carefully cut out the printed decals, discarding the background material. If you're using pressed leaves and flowers, select one or more for each bar of soap.

2. Select bars of soap that are as close to perfect as possible. Trim any uneven edges on each bar and make certain that the surface which will receive the decal is smooth and even.

3. Place a small amount of paraffin in a clean, empty tuna can, then place the can in the frying pan. Pour 1 inch (2.5 cm) of water into the frying pan, and place the pan over low heat; paraffin is flammable at high temperatures. When the paraffin has melted, remove the pan from the heat. Then, using your paintbrush, apply a coat of paraffin to the back of a decal. While the paraffin is still soft, position the decal on the soap, taking care to center it properly. If you're using pressed leaves or flowers, brush a layer or two of paraffin onto the soap before applying the decal; don't skimp on the paraffin, or the soap will damage the plant material.

4. Brush several layers of hot paraffin over the top of the decal, making sure that its edges are well covered. As you do this, you'll note that the decal will begin to become less visible.

5. When the paraffin has cooled, apply some baby oil or mineral oil to a soft cloth or paper towel. Rub the cloth or towel over the decal vigorously. As you do this, the decal will gradually be revealed. Continue rubbing until the decal colors are vibrant again, taking care not to remove all the wax. The decal will dissolve as the soap is used.

EVER wonder about the origin of the term "soap opera"? When radio programs were first broadcast in North America, manufacturers of a variety of products realized right away that this new medium offered a tremendous advertising opportunity. Before long, major soap companies were sponsoring a variety of entertaining radio programs for housewives. These were broadcast in serial form—and with them, the concept of soap operas was born.

TO WRAP
OR NOT TO WRAP

Soaps that haven't been scented, whether they're basic hand-cut soaps or hand-milled soaps, don't need protective wrappings. The best way to store these bars is to stack them in a small cardboard box. Place the box in your linen closet or in a similar warm, dry place with good air circulation.

Scented soaps, on the other hand, should always be wrapped or their essential oils will dissipate. Plastic wrap is the best material for this purpose. For a more attractive appearance, you may also want to cover the plastic with one of the wrapping materials listed below.

Wrapping Materials

- Plastic wrap, colored or clear
- Waxed paper
- Plain white paper
- Sewn fabric or plain muslin bags
- Gift wrap
- Calico or other lightweight fabrics
- Corrugated cardboard

WHEN TO WRAP

Soaps must be completely dry before they're wrapped, or they may mildew, mold, or develop a rancid odor. As you know, however, it isn't always easy to gauge whether or not a soap has reached the correct stage of dryness. The key here is experience. Until you have that experience under your belt, test for dryness levels by wrapping a few soaps and waiting a week. Then unwrap the bars to see what they look like. Are they damp, or do they feel just as dry as when you wrapped them? If they're damp, let them dry out for a couple of weeks before rewrapping.

GIFT BASKETS AND OTHER HANDY PACKAGES

Packaging soaps is almost as fun as making them. Let your imagination run wild! Containers can range from baskets—available at most craft-supply stores—to items that have their own special uses. A bread pan, for example, makes a perfect gift container for a gourmet cook, and a clay pot will please any gardener.

Many materials make attractive fillers for your containers. Easter grass, shredded colored paper, excelsior, and Spanish moss or sheet moss will all work well.

To spruce up your gift packages, tuck in some additional bath items. Nail brushes, loofah sponges, sea sponges, fancy hand towels, soap dishes, soap holders, and pumice stones are all appropriate.

By all means embellish your basket or package by adding yarns, fabric trims, ribbons, metallic cording, lace, angel wrap, or raffia. And don't forget to include an information card in any basket of soaps that you plan to give away. On that card, offer instructions on how to perform an allergen test (see page 29) and let the recipient of your gift basket know that dyed soaps should never be used to bathe infants (see page 25).

GIFT SOAP CONTAINERS

- Baskets of all shapes and sizes
- Wooden or metal trays
- Small bowls
- Gift boxes
- Wooden boxes
- Decorative plates
- Clay, porcelain, or ceramic flower pots
- Loaf pans
- Mixing bowls
- Cake pans
- Muffin tins
- Metal tins
- 1 to 2-pound (454 to 908 g) cocoa or spice tins
- Large shells
- Attractive glassware, old or new
- Brandy snifters
- Milk-glass containers
- Candy jars

SOAP DISPLAYS

Today, there are many craft shows, fairs, farmer's markets, and other venues that allow the home-based soap maker the opportunity to sell his or her wares. To take full advantage of these sales opportunities, your display of soaps should be tidy and attractive, of course, but should also "announce" immediately that you are selling hand-crafted soaps.

Displays that are straightforward in design, such as a single large box divided into compartments, will be much more effective than displays filled with many small containers. Buyers can be confused when they're faced with a multitude of soap-filled baskets! A single box will allow you display your soaps in an organized fashion.

Before you design your display, list the types of soap you'll be selling and make note of their shapes and sizes. Then decide how to distinguish one type of soap from another if their shapes and colors are the same, how to price your products, and how to educate your customers as to the special characteristics of each type of soap.

Shown in the photo (above) is a simple, country-style display specifically designed for soaps. Unless you possess the skills to build your own display, you will need to consult with a craftsperson who can execute your design. Before you make up your mind, talk with a few craftspeople; they often have valuable ideas to share, and they know the limitations of their craft much better than you do! Good luck selling!

Conversion Charts

Weights

This convenient chart will help speed up the process of weighing your ingredients. All amounts are rounded. Don't forget that the chart refers to weights only – never fluid ounces. All measurements in this book are given in weights, not in volumes.

OUNCES	POUNDS	GRAMS
8 ounces	1/2 pound	226 grams
16 ounces	1 pound	454 grams
24 ounces	1-1/2 pounds	679 grams
32 ounces	2 pounds	907 grams
40 ounces	2-1/2 pounds	1.1 kilograms
48 ounces	3 pounds	1.4 kilograms
56 ounces	3-1/2 pounds	1.6 kilograms
64 ounces	4 pounds	1.8 kilograms
72 ounces	4-1/2 pounds	2.0 kilograms
80 ounces	5 pounds	2.3 kilograms
88 ounces	5-1/2 pounds	2.5 kilograms
96 ounces	6 pounds	2.7 kilograms

Weights

0.035 ounces	1 gram
1 ounce	28.35 grams
1 pound	453.6 grams

Volumes

1 fluid ounce	29.6 ml
1 pint	473 ml
1 quart	946 ml
1 gallon (128 fl. oz.)	3.785 l

Temperatures

To convert Fahrenheit to Celsius: Subtract 32, multiply by 5, and divide by 9.

To convert Celsius to Fahrenheit: Multiply by 9, divide by 5, and add 32.

Linear

Readers who prefer to work in metric linear measurements will find the following charts useful.

INCHES	CM	INCHES	CM
1/8	0.3	20	50.8
1/4	0.6	21	53.3
3/8	1.0	22	55.9
1/2	1.3	23	58.4
5/8	1.6	24	61.0
3/4	1.9	25	63.5
7/8	2.2	26	66.0
1	2.5	27	68.6
1-1/4	3.2	28	71.1
1-1/2	3.8	29	73.7
1-3/4	4.4	30	76.2
2	5.1	31	78.7
2-1/2	6.4	32	81.3
3	7.6	33	83.8
3-1/2	8.9	34	86.4
4	10.2	35	88.9
4-1/2	11.4	36	91.4
5	12.7	37	94.0
6	15.2	38	96.5
7	17.8	39	99.1
8	20.3	40	101.6
9	22.9	41	104.1
10	25.4	42	106.7
11	27.9	43	109.2
12	30.5	44	111.8
13	33.0	45	114.3
14	35.6	46	116.8
15	38.1	47	119.4
16	40.6	48	121.9
17	43.2	49	124.5
18	45.7	50	127.0
19	48.3		

ACKNOWLEDGEMENTS

I would like to thank
the businesses and individuals listed below
for their contributions to
The Complete Soapmaker:
Tips, Techniques & Recipes
for Luxurious Handmade Soaps.

FOR THEIR GENEROUS CONTRIBUTIONS
OF MATERIALS:

The Candlewick Company
(New Britain, Pennsylvania)

The Essential Oil Company
(Lake Oswego, Oregon)

Frontier Herbs
(Norway, Iowa)

Lorann Oils
(Lansing, Michigan)

Pourette Manufacturing Company
(Seattle, Washington)

FOR THEIR DONATIONS
OF TIME, ADVICE, AND MATERIALS:

Phyllis Bernet
Janice Buckner
Junior Carter
Lois Favalo
Loie Mechetti
Marianne Ralbovsky
Jack Roubie
Loree Schader
Jane Taylor
Terry Taylor
Lisa Trumble
Olga White
Laura Wight

FOR THEIR REMARKABLE SKILLS:

Art Director, Chris Bryant
Photographer, Evan Bracken
Editor, Chris Rich

FOR HIS ENDLESS PATIENCE:

Dennis Coney

INDEX

INDEX TO RECIPES

Special thanks to Pourette Manufacturing Company of Seattle, Washington.
This manufacturer and distributor of candle and soap making supplies (wholesale and retail)
contributed generously toward the creation of this book.